Patricia O'Flaherty

BAKING

with
A Touch of Magic

100 MAGICAL BAKES

Copyright © A Touch of Magic by Patricia O'Flaherty 2021.
978-1-912328-99-4

All rights reserved.

No part of this book may be copied, reproduced, stored or transmitted in any way including any written, electronic, recording, or photocopying without written permission of the author and publisher. Although every precaution has been taken to verify the accuracy of the information contained herein, the author and publisher assume no responsibility for any errors or omissions. The rights for images used remain with the originator. The language used in this publication is flowery and filled with Patricia's typical casual irishisms she uses in her expressions around all things-baking/cooking and is not to be taken literally! Also note that your baking efforts may turn out different to those shown in the images. They are presented for demonstration purposes only. This is meant to be a fun baking book and is to be treated as such. Please do your own due diligence.

Published in Ireland by Orla Kelly Publishing.
Photography and text by Patricia O'Flaherty of www.atouchofmagic.ie.
Designed by Doodle Creative.

Hello!

I'm a busy mum of four and always developing fun recipes, baking cakes and teaching my craft is what I love to do. When lockdown hit on the 13th of March, I knew I had to do something to keep my kids entertained and save my sanity... I'll just bake!

I decided to start a Facebook live baking show every morning for all those isolating in their own homes, to help lighten the anxiety levels and share my love of traditional bakes to a country in lockdown.

Trying to get my kids up to establish some sort of daily routine during lockdown was like nailing jelly to a wall! But, I persevered and each morning either Lucy or Sophie would take it in turn to film my class and were rewarded with food!

In a nutshell, this book is dedicated to all those who whisked, cracked, walloped and smashed their way through all my recipes during lockdown and kept smiling. Had it not been for your continuous support, I would never have written this book.

Encouraged by you all, I've put together some of your favourites and created your family friendly book of escapism. There are over 100 simple recipes to enjoy. So when things get tough, or your nerves get frazzled, keep those cake tins full, and bring out a soothing cuppa to enjoy with your family.

But don't forget to …

"CLEAN AS YOU GO!"

Big love and massive thanks to my "everything"
Kieran, Katie, Lucy, Sophie, Darragh and my crazy twin sister Dee! ♡ ♡

Contents

COOKIES & BISCUITS

Bourbon Biscuits	1
Chocolate Chip Cookies	2
Coconut & Oat Cookies	3
Crazy Crinkle Cookies	4
Custard Creams	5
Gingerbread Men	6
Gingernuts	7
Italian Almond Cookies	8
Lemon & Thyme Shortbread	9
Pinwheel Cookies	10
Pizza Cookie	11
Protein Energy Bites	12
Red Velvet Cookies	13
Strawberry Cream Shortcake	14
Vanilla Sugar Cookie	15
Viennese Swirls	16

CUPCAKES & MUFFINS

Airy Fairy Almond Cupcakes	19
Banana & Walnut Caramel Cupcakes	20
Boston Cream Cupcakes	21
Chocolate Chip Muffins	23
Two Minute Chocolate Cupcakes	24
Coffee Cupcakes	25
Oreo Cupcakes	26
Raspberry Breakfast Muffins	27
Red Velvet Cupcakes	28
Tropical Coconut & Pineapple Muffins	29

BREADS, DOUGHS & PASTRY

Apple Turnover	33
Belgian Chocolate Caramel Tart	34
Breakfast Bagel Baps	35
Breakfast Filo Cups & Spicy Wedges	36
Chocolate Chip Soda Bread	37
Chocolate Ganache Tart	38
Cinnamon Rolls	39
Doughnuts	40
Focaccia Bread	41
French Fruit Galette	42
Hot Cross Buns	43
Irish Soda Bread	44
Naan Bread	45
Pizza Dough	46
Pop Tarts	47
Potato & Bluecheese Savoury Tart	48
Porridge Bread	49
Pretzels	50
Profiteroles	51
Puff Pastry Cones	52
Quiche Lorraine	54
Sausage Rolls	55
Treacle Bread	56
Twisted Milk Plait	57
Vegetarian Quiche	58

LOAF CAKES & TRADITIONAL BAKES

Apple & Mixed Berry Crumble	63
Banana Loaf	64
Battenburg Cake	65
Brown Scones	66
Carrot Cake	67
Courgette & Chocolate Chip Loaf	68
Chocolate & Vanilla Marble Loaf	69
Cinnamon Swirl Sponge	70
Cranberry & Orange Loaf	71
Fruit Cake	72
Gingerbread Cake	73
Jaffa Orange Jelly Cakes	74
Lemon Drizzle Cake	75
Lemon Meringue Pie	76
Lemon Poppy Seed Cake	78
Lemon Swissroll	79
Passion Fruit Roulade	80
Scones	81
Tea Brack	82
Victoria Sponge	83

TRAYBAKES & PARTY TREATS

Angel Cake	87
Baileys & White Chocolate Cheesecake	88
Belgian Chocolate Biscuit Cake	89
Berry Crumble Oat Bars	90
Berry & Banana Oat Pancakes	91
Berry Tiramisu	92
Black Forest Cherry Pavlova	93
Cake Pops	94
Caramel Squares	95
Chocolate Brownies	96
Chocolate Birthday Cake	97
Chocolate Mousse	98
Chocolate Tray Bake	99
Coffee Tiramisu	100
Crepes	101
Flapjack Jammy Oatbars	102
Granola Bars	103
Crunchie Honeycomb	104
Mango & Passion Fruit Ice-Cream	105
Marshmallow	106
Meringues	107
Mixed Berry Smoothie	108
Overnight Apple Cinnamon Porridge Oats	109
Penguin Sponge Cake	110
Strawberry Cheesecake	111
Tooty Fruity Traybake	112
Waffles	113

NOTE:

1. Baking soda, bicarbonate of soda and bread soda are all the same ingredient.
2. I use large eggs in most if not all of my recipes.
3. I use parchment paper to line my trays as it doesn't stick whereas greaseproof paper does.
4. I use 180C/350F/Gas 4 in most of the recipes.

COOKIES & BISCUITS

RISK IT FOR A BISCUIT! ♡ ♡

Bourbon Biscuits

INGREDIENTS

100g Caster Sugar
100g Butter
1 Large Egg
20g Cocoa powder
150g Plain flour
50g Birds custard powder

BUTTERCREAM FILLING

250g Icing sugar
125g Butter
2 tablespoons cocoa
1 tablespoons milk

METHOD

1. Pre heat oven to 180C/350F/Gas 4.
2. Line a tray with parchment paper. I use 12 inch x 9 inch.
3. Sieve all dry ingredients (flour, cocoa powder and custard powder) into a bowl.
4. Beat the butter and sugar together in the mixer and then add the egg.
5. Make sure you scrape down the bowl so everything is well blended.
6. Next add the dry ingredients and mix until combined.
7. Take the dough out of the bowl and roll out thinly. Remember these biscuits will be sandwiched together so don't make the biscuits too thick.
8. I roll out about ¼ inch thick first, then slightly roll out again so you have a thin base.
9. Cut into oblong fingers and place on the tray.
10. I used the end of a bamboo skewer to indent the signature holes you get on a bourbon or you can always purchase a cookie stamp for effect.
11. Place in the oven at 180C for 10-12 minutes.

FILLING

1. Add softened butter and icing sugar to a mixing bowl and beat for a few minutes until blended. Add a tablespoon of milk and continue to beat. If you need a little more, add a teaspoon at a time so the mixture is not too loose. Then add cocoa powder and beat for 5 minutes until you have a lovely soft buttercream.
2. The buttercream texture will depend on how warm or cold the butter is, so make sure it is at room temperature before you begin. Ideally leave it out of the fridge overnight as it makes for a delicious light buttercream.
3. The secret to buttercream is beating it vigorously for at least 5 minutes before you use. Always add the milk slowly to the buttercream as you may not need all the milk depending on the temperature of the butter.
4. Sandwich each biscuit with a good smear of chocolate buttercream and compress the biscuit so the buttercream oozes out the side. Using your finger or knife wipe off the excess so it seals the biscuit.

Put the kettle on and enjoy!

Chocolate Chip Cookie

INGREDIENTS

170g Butter (Soft Butter)
200g Dark brown sugar
125g Caster sugar
1 Large egg
1 Large egg yolk
350g Plain flour
½ teaspoon baking soda
200g Dark Chocolate 55% chips
1 teaspoon vanilla extract

Sieve the flour and baking soda before you add to the cookie dough so it's evenly mixed

METHOD

1. Pre heat oven to 180C/350 F/Gas 4.
2. Line a 12 x 9 inch tray with parchment.
3. In a mixer blend the butter and both sugars until mixed.
4. Add the vanilla extract.
5. Now add both the egg and egg yolk and beat until blended.
6. Scrape down the bowl and now add the flour and baking soda.
7. Finally add chocolate chips.
8. The mixture should be quite soft.
9. Use a tablespoon to scoop out the cookie dough the size of a large golf ball. I used a cookie scoop.
10. Put them in the oven in batches of 6 as they will spread during baking.
11. Bake them in the oven for 15 minutes until they are golden brown. Do not leave them in for any longer if you want the cookies to have a soft chewy bite.
12. They puff up in the oven but deflate when they come out.
13. Leave to rest and you will have crackled, chewy, crunchy cookies.

Absolutely Divine!

Coconut & Oat Cookies

INGREDIENTS

100g Butter
50g Soft brown sugar
50g Caster sugar
75g Plain Flour
½ tsp Baking Soda
120g Dark Chocolate chips 55%
75g Rolled oats
40g Coconut
1 Large egg

METHOD

1. Preheat oven to 180C/350 F/Gas 4.
2. Grease and line a baking tray. I use a 12 x 9 inch tray.
3. Weigh all ingredients so you're ready to crack on.
4. Beat butter and sugars together until smooth and creamy. Then this will take about a minute.
5. Add the egg, beat for a few seconds, stop mixer and scrape down batter from the sides.
6. Now add the flour and baking soda and blend for about a minute. Stop and make sure you scrape down the side of the bowl again until completely mixed together. You should have lovely sticky dough!
7. Add coconut and rolled oats. Stop the mixer and scrape down the bowl once again.
8. Finally add chocolate chips. Stir them in to the cookie mix using a spatula.
9. Using slightly damp hands, take a teaspoon of the mixture and roll in your hands. Flatten each cookie and place onto the baking tray. It's a sticky dough!
10. Bake for 10 minutes until golden brown. Leave on baking tray just for a minute or two as they are too soft to remove. The smell will be divine in your kitchen!
11. Use a spatula to lift them onto wire rack to cool and then devour!

Allow cool…then devour!

Crazy Crinkle Cookies

INGREDIENTS
(MAKES 10)

100g Melted Dark Chocolate (55%)
30g Melted Salted butter
1 large egg
55g Dark brown sugar
45g Plain flour
¼ teaspoon Baking powder
¼ teaspoon Bread soda
½ teaspoon vanilla extract
100g Dark chocolate (55%) chips

METHOD

1. Pre-heat oven to 180C/350F/Gas4 and line the cookie tray with parchment paper. I use a 12 x 9 inch tray.
2. Whisk the egg and brown sugar until light and fluffy. Takes about 3-4 minutes in a mixer.
3. While you're waiting, melt the chocolate and butter. I like to melt my chocolate first in the microwave for about 2 minutes in one minute intervals and leave rest until you melt the butter.
4. Do the same with the butter but with one 40 second burst, just enough to melt and then combine the two.
5. Pour the melted butter in on top of the melted chocolate and combine until mixed thoroughly.
6. At this stage the egg and sugar mix should have changed colour to a light coffee colour and whipped to a soft mousse like batter.
7. Pour the melted chocolate and butter mixture into the egg mixture and continue whisking at slow speed until blended.
8. Combine all the dry ingredients and then sprinkle in on top of the egg and sugar mix.
9. Using a spatula you can scrape down the bowl and stir in the chocolate chips.
10. Leave the cookie mixture now in the fridge to chill and do it's "thang" for at least 20-30 minutes.
11. Using a cookie scoop, scoop out some cookie dough and dollop on to the tray.
12. You should have four or five cookies per tray, well spaced out as they spread during baking.
13. Do not flatten the cookies once out of the scoop as they will flatten themselves as they bake.
14. Place in the pre-heated oven for no longer than 11-12 minutes. You want that soft "scrumpdiddlyumptious" centre and crinkle crunch on the outside.
15. Once out of the oven, leave on the tray for 2 minutes as these are very soft and floppy when first taken out.
16. You will go crazy waiting for these cookies to cool but wait....wait for them.
17. Transfer the cookies to a rack and leave cool for 15 minutes before you dive head first into one.

Custard Creams

INGREDIENTS
150g Plain Flour
150g Soft Butter
50g Custard Powder
50g Icing sugar
1/4 teaspoon Bicarbonate of soda

BUTTERCREAM FILLING
60g Soft Butter
120g Icing sugar
1 teaspoon vanilla extract

METHOD

1. Beat the butter and sugar until light and fluffy.
2. Scrape down the sides of the bowl.
3. Add the flour, bicarbonate of soda and custard powder and mix until completely blended.
4. The dough is very soft and will need to be chilled before rolling out.
5. Wrap the dough in clingfilm and place in the fridge to chill for 30 minutes.
6. Pre-heat the oven to 180C/350F/Gas4.
7. Once the dough is chilled roll out to a ¼ inch thickness and cut out using a scone cutter or biscuit cutter of choice.
8. Bear in mind the thickness of the biscuit has to be relatively thin as you will be sandwiching the biscuits together.
9. As I cut out the biscuits I place them on a tray in the fridge to keep them chilled while I finish cutting out the remainder of the dough.
10. Place on a greased tray and bake for 8 minutes.
11. Once baked, transfer to a cooling rack.
12. Top one side the biscuit with the vanilla buttercream and sandwich together.

BUTTERCREAM

Beat the very soft butter and icing sugar together. Add a teaspoon of vanilla extract and beat until combined. Place into a piping bag ready to sandwich the custard creams.

Trish's Top Tip

You can substitute custard powder with cornflour and make as instructed. These make the traditional biscuit treats seen in every Irish bakery! Sandwich with raspberry jam and decorate with some glacé icing and sprinkles.

Gingerbread Men

INGREDIENTS
(MAKES 12)

250g Plain Flour
75g cold butter (diced)
1½ teaspoons mixed spice
1½ teaspoons Ginger
1 teaspoon Bicarbonate of soda
100g Brown Sugar
1 large egg
50g Golden syrup

ICING

1 egg white
250g Icing sugar

METHOD

1. Pre-heat oven to 180C/350F/Gas4 and line a 12 x 9 inch baking tray with parchment.
2. Put about half the flour and all the butter in a food processor and whizz until it resembles fine breadcrumbs.
3. Tip the buttery flour mix into a large bowl and add the rest of the dry ingredients, the rest of the flour, spices, bicarbonate of soda and stir in the sugar.
4. Whisk the eggs with the golden syrup and then pour on top of the dry mix. Use the wooden spoon or mixer to combine together to make a yummy dough.
5. You can use the dough straight away or cover and chill or even freeze to use at a later date.
6. Roll out a quarter of the dough at a time so you don't over work the dough.
7. I like to roll out my cookie dough on Marzipan 'Spacers' which are like thick rulers especially used for cookie dough. As you roll out the dough between these train tracks all the cookies have the same thickness and will bake evenly.
8. If you don't have spacers, use a thin chopping board or cake board on either side as you roll to give a similar effect.
9. Cut out the cookies making sure you handle them with care as the dough is quite soft.
10. Place on a greased baking tray or lined parchment and ensure the cookies are well spaced before baking.
11. Bake for 12-15 minutes. The longer you leave them the crunchier they bake.
12. These cookies puff a little while baking but settle down once baked.
13. Make sure you have enough space on the tray for them to grow a little as they need wriggle room.

DECORATIVE ICING

14. To make the icing, beat the icing sugar with the egg white until you have a stiff paste, adding a little water a drop at a time where necessary if the icing is too stiff.
15. Fill a piping bag with the icing and snip a small cut at the tip so you have control of the piping.

Trish's Top Tip

The icing takes about an hour to set on each gingerbread man so be careful when packaging, that the gingerbread men are dry before you wrap.

Gingernuts

INGREDIENTS

125g Butter (room temp)
225g Caster Sugar
280g Self-raising Flour
1 tablespoon Ground ginger
1 teaspoon Bicarbonate of soda
1 large egg
2-3 tablespoons Golden syrup (I used 3 for a crunchier biscuit)

METHOD

1. Pre-heat the oven to 180C/350F/Gas4.
2. Line a 12 x 9 inch tray with parchment (makes life easier).
3. Mix the dry ingredients, flour, ginger, bicarbonate etc in a bowl.
4. Beat the sugar, butter and golden syrup until mixed, then add the egg and finally the dry flour ingredients.
5. Using a small ice cream scoop or melon baller, scoop out some cookie dough.
6. Place 6 cookies four fingers apart on the cookie tray.
7. Leave plenty of room as these cookies will spread.
8. Bake for 15 minutes but check after 12 minutes and remove if they are golden brown.
9. They puff up while they bake but collapse when they are removed from the oven to cool.
10. Leave on the tray for about a minute before you move them as the cookie dough is very soft and floppy. They firm up as they cool.
11. Place on a rack to cool completely while you click the kettle on for a brew!

Perfect Match!

Italian Almond Cookies

INGREDIENTS
(MAKES 20)

GLUTEN FREE & *DAIRY FREE*

200g Ground almonds
200g Caster sugar
2 Large egg whites
¼ teaspoon Cream of Tartar
1 teaspoon Almond extract
(Use ½ teaspoon if subtle flavour wanted)
100g Icing Sugar (for rolling only)

METHOD

1. Preheat the oven to 160C/320F/Gas3. Line a 12 x 9 inch baking tray with parchment.
2. Whip the egg whites in a clean bowl until soft peaks, just like a soft meringue 'Alfalfa'.
3. In another bowl blend the ground almonds and caster sugar together and mix until combined.
4. Add the stiffened egg white and almond extract to the dry ingredients and mix together to form a soft sticky dough.
5. Lightly dust your hands with icing sugar. I use a small ice cream scoop like a melon ball scooper or teaspoon and portion into mini golf balls.
6. Scoop some cookie dough into your hands and roll into a bowl, then roll into the icing sugar.
7. Put the cookies on a non stick baking parchment or silicon mat and bake for 25 minutes or until they are just barely golden and crackled on top.
8. Let them cool on a wire rack and devour!!!
9. These are sweet Italian amaretti style cookies, soft and chewy reminiscent of eating pure marzipan so a strong coffee makes a perfect match!

Put the kettle on and enjoy!

Lemon & Thyme Shortbread

INGREDIENTS

115g Soft Butter
70g Caster sugar
Zest of one large lemon
1 tablespoon fresh squeezed lemon juice
1 tablespoon fresh thyme leaves (finely chopped)
170g Plain Flour

METHOD

1. Pre-heat oven to 180C/350F/Gas4. Line a 12 x 9 inch tray with parchment paper.
2. Beat the butter and sugar together until soft and fluffy.
3. Scrape down the bowl, next add lemon zest, chopped thyme and lemon juice.
4. Finally gradually add the flour spoon by spoon until completely combined.
5. Turn the dough out onto a floured worktop and gently roll into a ball, slightly flatten and roll out.
6. If the dough is a little sticky, cover in clingfilm and chill for ten minutes in the fridge.
7. Roll the dough out between two cookie spacers* or roll ¼ inch thick. Shape using your favourite cookie cutter, I use a 2" love heart cookie cutter.
8. Transfer the cookies to the tray and bake for 10 minutes or if chilled maybe 12 minutes until the edges are golden brown.
9. Remove from the oven and transfer the cookies to a wire rack to cool.

* Just like we used for the gingerbread men to keep the cookies an even thickness.

Absolutely Divine!

Pinwheel Cookies

INGREDIENTS
100g Butter (Salted)
100g Caster sugar
1 egg yolk (large)
2 teaspoons vanilla extract
1 tablespoons milk
200g Plain Flour
1 teaspoon baking powder

CHOCOLATE PASTE:
20g cocoa mixed with 15g melted butter and 1 tablespoon of milk

METHOD

1. Pre-heat oven to 180C/350F/Gas4 and line cookie tray.
2. Melt 15g of butter in 1 tablespoon of milk for a few seconds in the microwave. Add cocoa and mix well. Set aside.

   PASTE
3. Cream butter and sugar until light and fluffy. Add the egg yolk, vanilla extract, then milk, and mix well until all are combined.
4. Mix the flour together with the baking powder and gradually add the dry ingredients, until the dough leaves the side of the bowl. Divide dough, (it weighs approximately 450g in total.) You want to weigh out 150g of dough to add to the chocolate paste and then the remaining 300g is for the vanilla cookie.
5. Add the chocolate paste to the weighed out vanilla (150g) and put it back in the mixing bowl to beat until the chocolate mixture is fully incorporated. This now forms the chocolate dough.
6. Form the vanilla and chocolate dough into flattened discs and wrap the cookie dough in cling wrap. Chill for about 10-15 minutes as it makes life easier when rolling out. Roll vanilla dough between clingfilm sheets into a rectangle around 7" in width and 8" in length. Repeat with the chocolate dough. Lay each dough side by side both still covered with clingfilm.
7. Peel back one sheet of clingfilm from both doughs and now flip the chocolate dough on to the vanilla dough. You'll end up with the chocolate on top of the vanilla dough with the clingfilm still attached, like a clingfilm sandwich.
8. With the clingfilm still on, lightly press the surface with a rolling pin. This helps stick both the vanilla and chocolate dough together, peel off remaining clingfilm. Trim the edges to tidy up...
9. With the short end facing you, roll the dough tightly into a log just like you would a swiss roll (Vanilla dough still has the clingfilm on its base to make it easier to roll up). Roll the dough in some sprinkles and chill in fridge for 30 minutes.
10. Slice about a finger thickness in width with a sharp knife.
11. Place cookie slices on a cookie sheet lined with parchment paper and bake for 10 - 12 minutes depending on the size. Check at 10 minutes. They should be baked, slightly puffed up and a little golden around the edges.
12. Remove cookies from tray and place on a cooling rack. Devour.

Trish's Top Tip

Once you split the dough, you can dye the vanilla cookie dough portion with gel paste if you wish and add a flavouring... so colour it green and add peppermint to make peppermint pinwheels! ..¼ teaspoon mint extract, squeeze of gel.

Pizza Cookie

INGREDIENTS
125g Plain Flour
1 teaspoon cornflour
1/2 teaspoon bicarbonate of soda
85g butter
75g Dark brown sugar
25g Caster sugar
1 Medium egg
100g dark chocolate chips

METHOD

1. Preheat oven to 180C/350F/Gas4.
2. Lightly grease an 8' sandwich tin.
3. Whisk together the flour, cornflour and bicarbonate of soda into a bowl.
4. Cream the butter and both sugars together until well blended.
5. Scrape down the sides of the bowl with the spatula to make sure it's all mixed together.
6. Now add the dry ingredients and then add the chocolate chips.
7. The mixture is a little soft and sticky, don't worry! Use the back of the spatula to blend or smooth the top of the cookie dough with wet hands.
8. Bake for 18-20 minutes or until puffed up and lightly browned on top...

Deeeeeelish!

Protein Energy Bites

INGREDIENTS
100g Oats
80g Coconut
50g Ground Flaxseed
80g Dark Chocolate Chips 55%
10g Awesome protein powder
165g Peanut Butter
80g Honey

METHOD

1. Weigh the dry ingredients in a bowl.
2. Add the peanut butter, honey and stir!
3. Blend all the ingredients until combined.
4. Take a tablespoon of the mixture and squeeze in your hands to compress.
5. Roll into a ball.
6. Each ball should weigh approximately 25g.
7. Makes approximately 22/24.
8. Chill in the fridge for 30 minutes to firm.

Red Velvet Cookies

INGREDIENTS
(MAKES 14)

115g Butter
100g Dark Brown sugar
70g Caster sugar
1 large Egg
1 teaspoon Vanilla extract
1 teaspoon of PROGEL red dye (gel or paste dye, NOT LIQUID)
200g Plain Flour
1 teaspoon Bicarbonate of soda
30g Cocoa powder
200g White chocolate chips

METHOD

1. Beat the butter and both sugars until light and fluffy.
2. Add the egg.
3. Scrape down the side of the bowl and add the vanilla extract and red food dye and blend.
4. Next add flour, bicarbonate of soda and cocoa powder until completely combined.
5. Finally add the white chocolate chips.
6. Let the cookie dough rest in the fridge to firm up for 15 minutes.
7. While you're waiting, pre-heat the oven to 180C/350F/Gas Mark 4 and line the cookie tray with parchment paper.
8. Scoop out the chilled cookie dough using a medium sized ice-cream scoop or large tablespoon or even use your fingers.
9. The cookies are the size of a golf ball. Roll the dough in your hands to create a ball of dough or if using an ice-cream scoop just leave as is when scooped out and dollop on to tray.
10. Place six cookies (four fingers apart) well spaced on a tray as they will spread when baking.
11. Bake for 10 minutes and remove from the oven and leave sit for 5 minutes before transferring to a rack to cool.
12. These cookies puff and then collapse while they cool so don't be tempted to cook for longer unless you want a firmer cookie.

Trish's Top Tip

The red dye is optional in this recipe and although it seems a lot it really isn't as you make 14 with this cookie batch.

Strawberry & Cream Shortcakes

INGREDIENTS
100g Butter
40g Caster sugar
150g Plain flour

STRAWBERRY COMPOTE
300g Fresh strawberries (hulled and halved)
100ml or approx 6 tablespoons maple syrup
4 tablespoons water

FILLING
175ml cream
2-4 tablespoons Greek yoghurt (your choice)
1 tablespoon sugar and Icing sugar for sprinkling

METHOD

1. Pre-heat the oven to 180C/350F/Gas4.
2. Beat the butter and sugar until light and fluffy and scrape down the sides of the mixing bowl before you add the flour.
3. Slowly work in the flour until smooth (you may have to add a splash of milk if needed but try not to).
4. Once the dough comes together, wrap in clingfilm and chill for 5-10 minutes.
5. While you're waiting for the dough to chill, put the strawberries in a pan, add the maple syrup and bring to the boil, then simmer for two minutes (set the timer).
6. Next using a slotted spoon, remove the strawberries after the two minute boil and increase the heat for 2-3 minutes until the liquid has reduced by two thirds. You want a light syrup.
7. Leave the syrup to cool.
8. Dust the work surface with a little flour and roll out the dough to ¼ inch thick, which is quite thin. You need to roll out these shortcakes thinly as you will be stacking with filling.
9. Using a 3" scone cutter stamp out 12 rounds and line the baking tray with parchment.
10. Bake in a pre-heated oven for 10-12 minutes until golden.
11. Scatter over 1 tablespoon caster sugar while the biscuits are still warm and leave cool completely

FILLING

1. In a bowl whip the cream to soft peaks and add the yoghurt.
2. Arrange the biscuits on a serving plate.
3. Top each biscuit with a dollop of the cream mix and spoon some of the delicious strawberry compote and a drizzle of the syrup.
4. Balance the remaining biscuit on top of the filling.
5. Ta-Dah you've got posh biscuits with a delicious strawberry and cream compote filling... anyone for tennis!

Trish's Top Tip

The hull or calyx is the green leafy top of the strawberry which is gennerally removed before cooking. Just use the tip of a knief or slice to remove.

Vanilla Sugar Cookies

INGREDIENTS
(MAKES 24 DEPENDING ON THE SIZE OF THE COOKIE CUTTER)
400g Plain Flour
200g Caster Sugar
200g Butter (cold)
1 Large egg

METHOD

1. Preheat the oven to 180C/350F/Gas 4.
2. Prepare the tray with parchment paper.
3. Beat the butter and the sugar with the beater until it resembles coarse sand.
4. Crack a large egg and add to the mix.
5. Slowly add the flour until all combined.
6. The dough is ready when it combines together.
7. Dust the worktop with a little flour and roll out the dough.
8. I use "spacers" to get an even depth.
9. Roll out the dough and use your favourite cookie cutters, make sure they are all the same size or they won't bake evenly. I used a 3" round cutter or have fun using a novelty cupcake cutter.
10. Chill for about 30 minutes in the fridge before baking.
11. Bake in the oven for 12-15 minutes depending on the oven.
12. When they have a golden glow around the edges, the cookies are done.
13. Leave to cool before you ice.
14. You can either dust with some icing sugar or ice with glacé icing.

These cookies are fantastic as they hold their shape well when baked. They have a crisp bite and a subtle hint of vanilla, perfect base for cookie decorating.

GLACE ICING

100g icing sugar mixed with a 2-3 teaspoons water, add a little liquid colour too if you like but make sure you add the colour first before you add the water so it doesn't get too runny!

To make these cookies GLUTEN FREE I tweak the recipe.... I add ½ teaspoon Xanthan gum, I use Dove Farm Gluten free flour and the butter is at room temperature. It makes binding easier and the cookies need at least an hour to chill in the fridge!

Viennese Swirls

INGREDIENTS
250g Very soft butter
50g Icing sugar
250g Plain flour
50g Cornflour
½ teaspoon vanilla extract

BUTTERCREAM FILLING
100g Butter (Soft)
200g icing sugar
½ teaspoon vanilla extract or almond extract
75g Seedless Jam or lemon curd (optional)
1 tablespoon milk

METHOD

1. Pre heat the oven to 180C/350F /Gas Mark 4 and line a baking tray with parchment paper.
2. Put the butter in the mixer and beat for a minute until nice and soft, followed by the icing sugar. Add the vanilla extract, then flour, cornflour and beat until a soft paste.
3. You need the cookie paste to be quite soft as you will need to pipe it … if the paste is too stiff you will not be able to pipe, so make sure you beat the paste long enough about 2 minutes on medium speed. Scrape out the mixture from the bowl and fill a piping bag with an open star nozzle.
4. Pipe 3' long strips of cookie paste across the tray and space them well apart as they do spread a little when baking. You'll get loads of Viennese fingers from this or pipe swirls if you're feeling adventurous.
5. It's important to chill the cookies for at least 30 minutes as they hold their distinct shape better once chilled.
6. Bake in the oven for 10-12 minutes depending on the size of the cookies. Check the cookies after 10 minutes, you should have a lovely golden hue.
7. Cool on a rack while you make the filling, be careful as they are still very delicate.

FILLING

1. Put all the ingredients into the mixer and beat the living daylights out of it for at least a minute. You'll see the colour change from a buttery yellow to a pale cream.
2. Using a piping bag you can pipe a trail of buttercream on one half of the Viennese swirl, then sandwich with another on top. I love to then dip the tip one side with dark melted chocolate and leave to set on a tray.
3. For the traditional Viennese Swirl, put a little raspberry jam on the base of one swirl and pipe some buttercream on another and sandwich together and dust with some icing sugar to finish.

KA-BOOM…. Afternoon Tea anyone …#sorted

CUPCAKES & MUFFINS

PROCRASTIBAKING

When you have a million things to do,
but ignore everything and bake

Airy Fairy Almond Cupcakes

INGREDIENTS
(MAKES 12)

200g Caster Sugar
200g Self-Raising Flour
200g Butter (Very soft)
4 large eggs
1 teaspoon baking powder
½ teaspoon Almond extract
40g Ground Almonds
(All above ingredients at room temperature!)

BUTTERCREAM

250g Soft Butter
500g Icing Sugar
2-3 tablespoons milk (Start with two, you may not need it depending on how soft the butter is)

METHOD

1. Preheat the oven to 180C/350F/Gas 4.
2. Fill a 12 cupcake tray with cases.
3. Beat the butter and sugar for a minute or two until completely blended.
4. Add the almond extract and mix again.
5. Now add the flour and baking powder (sounds daft but it prevents the mix splitting).
6. Gradually add the eggs one by one and mix until combined. Scrape down the mixer to make sure it is all blended and you have a smooth batter.
7. Using an ice-cream scoop or spoon, scoop or dollop the batter and fill the cases 2/3 up and pop in the oven. Watch those beauties rise!
8. Bake for 20 minutes possibly 25 minutes depending on the oven.
9. Once baked, cool on a rack for a few minutes before dusting with a cloud of icing sugar. You can also use buttercream if you wish but I love the simplicity of the dusting as you can taste the background flavour of almond and its discreet sweetness.
10. If however you are an icing fiend, decorate with piped buttercream.

BUTTERCREAM

Beat the living daylights out of the buttercream for at least five minutes, until icing has changed to a pale colour. Smear or pipe a swirl on the cupcake and devour!

Devour!

Banana & Walnut Caramel Muffins

INGREDIENTS
(MAKES 24 CUPCAKES)
350g Self-raising Flour
175g Brown sugar
1 teaspoon Bicarbonate of soda
2 teaspoons mixed spice
100g Walnuts
4 Large eggs
1 teaspoon vanilla extract
200ml Sunflower oil
200g Mashed banana (2-3 bananas)
100g Crushed Pineapple (Tin of drained chunks weighed and blitzed)
Juice of one orange

FILLING
One tin of Carnation caramel sauce
Whipped Italian meringue
Buttercream for piping
Chopped walnuts (for decorating)
Toffee nibs (for decorating)

BUTTERCREAM
6 Egg whites
200g Caster sugar
1 teaspoon cream of tartar
60mls water
500g Unsalted NOT SALTED

METHOD

1. Pre-heat the oven to 180C/350F/Gas 4. Line 24 cupcake cases in the cupcake tray.
2. In a large bowl add the dry ingredients, flour, bread soda, spices, walnuts and brown sugar.
3. In a jug whisk together the oil, eggs, pineapple, orange juice, vanilla extract and mashed banana.
4. Add the wet ingredients to the dry mix and stir until completely blended.
5. Using an ice cream scoop, scoop the batter and fill the cases to 2/3 full. Bake for 20 minutes.
6. Once baked remove and cool on a rack.

ITALIAN MERINGUE BUTTERCREAM

7. Add 60ml of water to a saucepan along with the sugar.
8. Mix well before you turn the heat on. It's important not to stir the pot once the heat starts.
9. Brush the inside of the pan around the water level at the base of the pan to prevent the sugar from crystallising.
10. Now let it bubble away for at least 5 minutes until it hits a temperature of 112C soft ball stage. Swirling the pot at intervals to prevent hot spots, DO NOT STIR.
11. While the sugar syrup is doing it's "thang" whisk 6 egg whites in a large mixing bowl and whip until you have soft peaks. Sprinkle in the cream of tartar which helps stabilise the egg whites.
12. Once the sugar has reached temperature, take it off the heat and slowly pour the sugar syrup onto the egg whites while still slowly whisking.
13. I pour from an extended height as it cools the sugar syrup down faster and speeds up the process.
14. This will take at least 20 minutes to whip and cool down before you add the unsalted butter.
15. Piece by piece add the softened butter, until you end up with what looks like soft whipped cream.
16. You will know it's done when it comes together in a smooth soft buttercream ready to pipe.
17. I use a 1M Wilton nozzle and fill a piping bag. Swirl buttercream and sprinkle with chopped walnuts and toffee nibs.

Boston Cream Cupcakes

INGREDIENTS
(MAKES 12)
BATTER
90g Really soft butter
155g Caster sugar
90g Sour cream (room temp)
2 teaspoon vanilla extract
3 Large egg whites
160g Plain flour
2 teaspoons Baking powder
100ml Milk

PASTRY CREAM
80g Caster sugar
12g Cornflour
2 Egg Yolks
15g Butter
1 teaspoon Vanilla extract
270ml Milk

CHOCOLATE GANACHE
300g Dark chocolate chips 55%
30ml Glucose (golden syrup will do at a pinch)
200ml cream

METHOD

1. Pre-heat the oven to 180C/350F/Gas 4 and line the cupcake tray with cases.
2. Mix the flour and baking powder in a bowl and set aside.
3. Starting with the batter, beat the living daylights out of the soft butter and sugar for a few minutes until it's light, fluffy and changes colour. (It will be paler).
4. Stop the mixer and scrape down the sides, next add the sour cream to the mix, followed by the vanilla extract and mix until completely blended.
5. While the mixer is running, pour in half of the egg whites to give them a chance to volumize (posh word for bulking up so they become nice, fluffy and airy!) then add the remaining egg whites.
6. Next add in the dry ingredients, alternating between the flour and milk until combined.
7. Ka-Boom the cupcakes are ready to transfer to the cupcake tray.
8. I use an ice-cream scoop to make things easier. Dollop the batter into each case and bake for 15-18 minutes. Just remember the cupcakes will continue to cook in the residual heat in the cupcake tray so try not to overbake.
9. Remove cupcakes and transfer to a cooking rack to chill and relax like a true Bostonian!!

See the recipe for pastry cream and chocolate ganache on the next page.

Boston Cream Continued ->

PASTRY CREAM (POSH CUSTARD)

1. Place the caster sugar, cornflour and milk in a saucepan and blend. Stir the mixture and bring to a gentle boil and cook for two minutes. This activates the cornflour and thickens the mix. It now looks like wallpaper paste but don't panic, it's now a milk custard!
2. Take about 2-3 tablespoons of the hot milk custard and slowly add to the egg yolks so you temper the egg mix. "Tempering" is just a fancy way of saying that you want to mix two liquids of different temperatures together without altering the texture of the liquids. Oooooo… Fancy!
3. Next slowly put the egg yolk mixture back into the saucepan with the milk custard and stir. Bring it back to cook for another two minutes which cooks the egg. Then add the vanilla extract.
4. Once the mixture comes to a slow bubble, turn off the heat and add the butter. The mixture will have a lovely glossy sheen. Ka-Boom Custard made!
5. Transfer to a bowl to cool and cover with clingfilm to prevent a skin forming. It will take a few hours to cool before it's ready to pipe.

GANACHE

6. Heat the cream to boiling point, and wait about 10 seconds before pouring over the chocolate. Leave to settle for about a minute before gently stirring. Add the glucose to the chocolate soup (this adds a shine) and stir until completely mixed through with no lumps and bumps. If there are any lumps of unmelted chocolate just zap in microwave with ten second intervals. Leave to set for a few hours.

ASSEMBLY

7. Fill two piping bags one with custard filling and the other fitted with an open star nozzle with the chocolate ganache.
8. Using the tip of a nozzle stab each cupcake and as you do you, create a cavity in which to fill the pastry cream/custard. The bigger the hole the more custard filling you can get into your gob!
9. Inject each cupcake with a generous squeeze of pastry cream so it oozes to the top of the cupcake and fills the cavity as you squeeze.
10. Next pipe a generous swirl of the ganache filling.
11. You have now passed cupcake college and made your first Boston Cream cupcakes, ready to take on the world!

Knock your " SOX " off!

Chocolate Chip Muffins

INGREDIENTS
(MAKES 10 CUPCAKES)

200g Granulated sugar
60g Melted butter
60ml Sunflower Oil
1 large egg
1 Egg white
1 teaspoon Vanilla extract
150ml Buttermilk
220g Plain Flour
2 teaspoons Cornflour
2 teaspoons baking powder
150g Dark chocolate chips 55%

TOPPING

25g Granulated sugar
(used to sprinkle top of cupcakes)

METHOD

1. Pre-heat the oven to 190C/375F/Gas 5.
2. Prepare the cupcake tray with tulip cases or large muffin cases.
3. Get a large bowl and add the melted butter, oil and sugar, mix until blended.
4. Next add the egg and egg white and gently whisk. Pour in the buttermilk and vanilla extract.
5. Sprinkle half the flour on top of the wet mixture and stir slowly followed by the remaining flour.
6. Finally add the chocolate chips and gently stir into the mixture taking care not to over mix.
7. Now crazy as this sounds, leave the batter sit, covered with a clean T-towel for 15 minutes.
8. You can "clean as you go" and wash all the containers while you wait!
9. Next scoop out the batter using an ice-cream scoop and dollop into the cupcake tray.
10. Sprinkle with a little granulated sugar to create a crunchy top!
11. Bake in the preheated oven for 8 minutes (set the timer!) After 8 minutes, without opening the oven, turn the oven down to 180C/350F/Gas 4 and continue to bake for a further 12 minutes.
12. Once they have baked take them out and let the residual heat continue to cook these gorgeous muffins.
13. Transfer to a cooling rack and wait 5 minutes before you nose dive into a muffin! (Please don't linetally nose dive! That would smell disaster! LOL)

Nose dive in!

Two Minute Chocolate Cupcakes

INGREDIENTS
(MAKES 12)

175g Butter (Very soft)
165g Brown sugar
115g Self-raising Flour
1 teaspoon baking powder
3 Large eggs
½ teaspoon vanilla extract

COCOA PASTE*

40g Cocoa powder
4 tablespoons buttermilk (milk will do or even water)
Blend 4 tablespoons of buttermilk in with the cocoa powder to create a paste, it makes it easier to blend in the mixer and also doesn't dry out the batter.

ICING

60g Butter (Melted)
30g Cocoa Powder
3 tablespoons milk
250g Icing sugar

METHOD

1. Preheat the oven to 180C/350F/Gas 4.
2. Prepare and fill the cupcake tray with cases.
3. Put all the ingredients along with the cocoa paste* in the mixer and blend for about a minute until incorporated.
4. KA-BOOM!!! Cupcakes made.
5. Using an ice cream scoop, dollop some batter into each cupcake case and make sure you scrape out the bowl completely so nothing left... nothing for Mr. Manners in the bowl... no licking.
6. Place the cupcake tray into the preheated oven for 20 minutes and the kitchen will smell of deliciousness........
7. Using the same bowl, throw in all the icing ingredients and again blend until mixed through.
8. Once the cupcakes have baked, cool on a wire rack for 30 minutes before piping with the buttercream and decorating as you please.

Enjoy... #micdrop

Coffee Cupcakes

INGREDIENTS
200g Caster Sugar
200g Soft Butter
200g Self-Raising Flour
4 Eggs (Large)
3 tablespoons Buttermilk (or milk will do)
2 tablespoons Espresso powder
1 teaspoon Vanilla Extract

GANACHE TOPPING
800g White chocolate drops
300ml Cream
1 tablespoon Espresso powder (two teaspoons water to dissolve

METHOD

1. Preheat the oven to 180C/350F/Gas 4 and prepare the cupcake tray with cases.
2. Place the soft butter in the mixer and add the caster sugar. Blend for a minute or two just so it combines together.
3. Next add the eggs one by one until completely mixed.
4. Stop the mixer and scrape down the bowl and at the same time add the flour alternating with the buttermilk- coffee mix.
5. Using a cupcake scoop, scoop the batter into the cupcake tray.
6. Bake for 20 minutes.
7. Allow the cupcakes to cool on a wire rack before icing.

GANACHE TOPPING

1. Bring the cream to boiling point and leave for 20 seconds before pouring over the white chocolate.
2. Leave for another 20 seconds before you stir. You will have a silky glossy chocolate ganache.
3. Make sure all the white chocolate nibs have melted, if not put back in the microwave and zap for 10 second intervals until the chocolate has melted. The residual heat will continue to melt the chocolate.
4. Add the dissolved espresso to the ganache and stir.
5. Leave the ganache to cool in the fridge for 30 minutes or longer if needs be and then whip until soft peaks form ready for piping.
6. Using a 1M Wilton nozzle, fill the piping bag and pipe away a swirl of delicious coffee ganache. Top with a chocolate coffee bean.

Put the kettle on and enjoy!

Oreo Cupcakes

INGREDIENTS

125g Plain Flour
30g Cocoa powder
1 teaspoon Baking powder
½ teaspoon Bicarbonate of soda
100g Brown sugar
100g Granulated sugar
80ml Sunflower oil
120ml Buttermilk
1 Large Egg
1 teaspoon vanilla extract
120ml Boiling water
1 teaspoon espresso powder or instant coffee granules (optional)

BUTTERCREAM ICING

230g Soft Butter
360g Icing sugar
30-45ml of cream (depends on how soft the butter is)
1 teaspoon vanilla extract
75g crushed Oreo biscuits
Mini Oreos for decoration (optional)

METHOD

1. Pre-heat the oven to 180C/350F/Gas4. Line the cupcake tray... Makes about 14-16 cupcakes.
2. In a large bowl add the dry ingredients, flour, baking powder, bicarbonate of soda, cocoa powder and sugars and blend making sure you have no lumps or bumps.
3. In a jug mix the oil, buttermilk, egg and vanilla extract.
4. Make up the espresso coffee using the 120ml of boiling water (if not using coffee you still need to add the 120ml of hot water without the coffee).
5. Whisk the dry ingredients together until completely blended and now add the buttermilk egg mixture and coffee mix and stir until smooth. You will have a very runny batter, like pancake batter but don't panic!
6. Fill the cupcake cases half way. You should fill between 14-16 cases.
7. Transfer to the preheated oven for 20 minutes or until a toothpick inserted into the centre of one cupcake comes out clean and the tops spring back when lightly touched. No Miss Piggy wallops!
8. Cool on a rack for 20 minutes before icing.

BUTTERCREAM

1. In the mixer soften the butter by beating on high for half a minute.
2. Next add all the icing sugar and beat that for another minute on high before you add the vanilla extract.
3. Scrape down the bowl and now slowly add the cream until the mix is pale and creamy.
4. Turn the mixer down and mix in the Oreo crushed biscuits on a low speed until well combined. Make sure the Oreos are finely crushed as they will be piped through a piping bag so need to be smooth and free of lumps.
5. Fit an open star nozzle on the piping bag and pipe a swirl of buttercream on the cupcakes once cooled.
6. Finish with a baby Oreo on top as decoration....

** Happy Lockdown 13th Birthday Sophie** #makingmemories #lockdownbirthday

Raspberry Breakfast Muffins

INGREDIENTS
(MAKES 9-12)

90ml Milk (Low fat)
90ml Sunflower oil
1 large egg
1/2 teaspoon vanilla extract
150g Self-Raising Flour
70g Caster sugar
1 teaspoon baking powder
50g Porridge oats
100g Frozen berries** or fresh if seasonal (See Tip)

METHOD

1. First pre-heat the oven to 180C/350F/Gas Mark 4.
2. Measure out all the ingredients so you have everything at hand.
3. Mix the milk, sunflower oil, egg and vanilla extract in a jug.
4. In a separate bowl add the flour, baking powder, oats.
5. Toss the berries into the flour mix before you add the sugar.
6. Add the wet ingredients to dry ingredients and gently stir. Don't over mix as you don't want to have heavy muffins. You want them as light as fairy wings!
7. Scoop the batter into each cupcake case using an ice cream scoop. You should get at least nine and can get more if using traditional cupcake cases.
8. To make them crunchy, sprinkle a little pinch of oats on top before they bake.
9. Bake for about 25 minutes.
10. Remove from tray and cool on baking rack for 5 minutes.
11. Leave for at least 20 minutes to cool as the fruit is very hot and will burn your mouth!!!! You have to be patient, they're worth the wait.

Trish's Top Tip*

Toss the frozen berries in flour before you mix into the muffin batter so they won't sink to the bottom of the case. They will still taste delicious!

Red Velvet Cupcakes & Marshmallow Topping

INGREDIENTS
(MAKES 12-16)

100g Very Soft butter
230g Caster Sugar
2 Eggs
250g Plain Flour
1 teaspoon baking soda
1 teaspoon baking powder
2 tablespoons of cocoa powder
200ml Warm buttermilk
1 25ml bottle of liquid food dye
1 teaspoon vanilla extract
1 teaspoon white wine vinegar (not malt/household.. That's for the chips!)

MARSHMALLOW MERINGUE TOPPING

200g Caster sugar
2 tablespoons water
2 tablespoons golden syrup
3 Egg whites
½ teaspoon cream of tartar (Helps stabilise the egg whites and gives great texture!)

METHOD

1. Pre-heat the oven to 180C/350F/Gas 4.
2. Line the cupcake tray with cupcake cases.
3. Place the very soft butter and sugar in the mixer and mix until smooth, takes about two minutes to change colour.
4. While you're waiting, blend all the dry ingredients together. Flour, cocoa powder, bread soda and baking powder.
5. I like to warm my buttermilk in the microwave for about 30 seconds so it mixes more easily with the flour blend and also activates the bread soda a little bit faster.
6. Blend the wet ingredients now into the warmed buttermilk, (red dye, vanilla extract and vinegar).
7. As the egg mix is blending in the mixer, slowly add the dry flour mix and alternate with the red buttermilk soup! Alternate between dry and wet mixes.
8. Let it blend for less than minute before you scrap down the bowl to make sure it's all mixed thoroughly.
9. Scoop out the batter using an ice-cream scoop as it makes life easier and also ensures that each cupcake bakes evenly and at the same time.
10. Bake in a pre-heated oven at 180C for 20-25 minutes.
11. Cool on a rack before you crack on with the marshmallow topping.

MARSHMALLOW MERINGUE TOPPING

1. Fill a saucepan with about an inch of water and sit a heatproof bowl on top making sure the bowl doesn't touch the bottom. Place the sugar, water, egg whites, and golden syrup into the bowl and turn on the heat. Stir for at least 5 minutes until you have cooked the egg whites and have a hot gelatinous goo!! Don't panic. It should look like that. You want the sugar to dissolve so you don't have a granular texture to the marshmallow!
2. You can test if its still grainy by rubbing a little of the egg goo between your fingers so it doesn't feel grainy before you tip into a clean mixing bowl.
3. Now whisk the meringue for 7 minutes in the mixer. As the meringue starts to cool, it will thicken up. Once the 7 minutes are up you're ready to rock and roll and fill the piping bag.
4. Make sure you work fast as the meringue sets quickly.
5. This mixture will fill 15 cupcakes.

Tropical Coconut & Pineapple Muffins

DRY INGREDIENTS
100g Plain Flour
1 ½ teaspoons baking powder
¼ teaspoon baking soda
50g finely chopped dried apricots (I used soft variety)
75g Castor Sugar
25g Coconut

WET INGREDIENTS
2 Large eggs (beaten)
120ml Sunflower oil
170g crushed pineapple (4 Rings of canned pineapple, blitzed!)
½ teaspoon vanilla extract (or coconut or almond extract)

METHOD

1. Pre heat the oven to to 180C/350F/Gas 4and line the cupcake tray.
2. Mix the flour, baking powder, baking soda, dried apricot, caster sugar and coconut.
3. Now add the wet ingredients (eggs, oil, pineapple and extract of choice) and fold into the mixture with a spatula making sure you don't over mix.
4. Ka-Boom you're done!!
5. Bake for 20-25 minutes.
6. Cool on a wire rack for 10 minutes and enjoy!

A GOOD BAKER WILL RISE TO THE OCCASION... IT'S THE 'YEAST' YOU CAN DO.

BREADS, DOUGHS & PASTRIES

BAKE THE WORLD A BETTER PLACE

Apple Turnovers

INGREDIENTS

3 large Brambly or Granny Smith apples
½ teaspoon cinnamon
½ teaspoon mixed spice
3 tablespoons Brown sugar
Egg for glazing
Jus-Rol Puff Pastry ready rolled sheet 320g

METHOD

1. Pre-heat the oven to 180C/350F/Gas 4.
2. Take the puff pastry out of the fridge 30 minutes before you use it.
3. Unroll the puff pastry and have the pastry long side facing you, like a large rectangle.
4. Cut in half across the width of the pastry cutting from left to right with a pizza wheel so you now have two even strips.
5. Fold the top left corner of the pastry to meet the bottom right of the pastry strip. It folds like a triangle.
6. Cut upwards to create your first triangle and when you open it out you have a square panel. Repeat across the strip until you have 6 square panels.
7. Fill a tablespoon of the mixture close to the centre and keep about an inch away from the edge so you keep the filling intact.
8. Brush with some beaten egg and seal the edges. Crimp with a fork and a light brush of glazed egg and Ka-Boom into the oven those beauties go!
9. 180C for 20 minutes until golden brown.
10. Once baked put on a cooling rack and sprinkle with a very generous dusting of icing sugar…. very generous… did I say generous .. It's all about the generous sugar, lol
11. Wait for at least 15 minutes before cracking into one of those beauties as the filling will be like mount Vesuvius … (look that up) and too hot!

FILLING

12. In a saucepan add the sliced apples, brown sugar, cinnamon and mixed spice and a squeeze of half a lemon.
13. Cook over a low medium heat, stirring as needed, for about 2 to 3 minutes so you're are not looking for the apples to cook all the way through. Just enough to allow some juice to release and flavours to mingle… who doesn't love to mingle.. lol
14. Stir in walnuts and raisins if you want at this stage for an extra crunch, remove from heat and set aside until completely cold. Adding the apples mixture to the pastry at this stage would make the pastry go soggy and nobody likes a soggy bottom! Wait until the apple mixture is completely cold before you assemble the apple turnovers.

Ka-Boom! You're done!

Belgian Chocolate Caramel Tart

INGREDIENTS
175g Plain Flour
100g cold butter (cut into pieces)
1 tablespoon Icing sugar
1 egg yolk
2 tablespoons ice cold water

FILLING
1 Can of Carnation caramel filling
200ml Cream
300g Belgian chocolate (55%) chips

METHOD
STEP 1 – THE PASTRY
1. Pre-heat the oven to 180C/350F/Gas4.
2. For the pastry, put the flour and cold butter into a bowl and blend between your fingers. The method I use is "Show me the money".
3. Blend the butter and flour between your fingertips and as you do, you flatten the butter into small pieces as it blends and disappears into the flour like breadcrumbs.
4. Next add the icing sugar at this stage and mix with your fingers.
5. Make a well in the centre of the flour butter mix and add the egg yolk.
6. Sprinkle the cold water around the bowl and use a butter knife to blend in a criss cross pattern across the bowl to represent the mixing blade. I don't use my hand until I can see the pastry come together in clumps, the colour changes too as the butter is mixed and egg yolk to a pale yellow.
7. Now's the time to go in with your hand like a claw and mix the dough. Keep your hand stiff. As you move around the bowl and the pastry will come together in a clump. You can start a gentle knead with your hand still in the bowl to bring the dough together.
8. Sprinkle some flour on the worktop and roll out you dough.
9. Now any normal person would let this pastry chill for 30 minutes but then again I'm not normal, lol.
10. Roll out the dough immediately to fit the round 9" flan tin. Using the rolling pin, roll up and down and move the pastry around, so up down and turn it around, so just think from 12 O'Clock to 6 O'Clock and twist the pastry each time so it doesn't stick on the worktop.
11. Use the rolling pin as a guide to roll the pastry back on to the rolling pin so you can lift in place and cover the tin. I use a 9" loose bottomed flan tin.
12. Prick the pastry base with a fork on the base and along the sides.
13. Now you can chill the pastry for 30 minutes to an hour to settle so the pastry doesn't shrink when baked. Pre-heat the oven while you're waiting....
14. Bake the pastry case "blind" which means place some foil directly onto the flan tin to create a blanket of foil and weigh down with either ceramic beans, dry beans or rice.
15. Bake for 15 minutes, then take out of the oven and remove the foil (be careful as the foil is hot and the beans are mobile!!!) and bake for another 5-8 minutes until the pastry is pale golden and cooked.

STEP 2. THE CARAMEL
16. When the pastry case is completely cold, fill with the prepared caramel filling, smooth with a platter knife or spoon right to the edges, no need to be super fussy as you are going to drown it with chocolate ganache!

STEP 3. GANACHE
17. Heat the cream in a small saucepan until just barely coming to a simmer or zap in the microwave for 1-2 minutes but keep an eye on it.
18. Pour hot cream over chopped chocolate and wait a minute before you stir. Now with a spatula mix until combined and smooth.
19. Pour into cooled tart shell on top of the caramel and allow to set overnight at room temperature or for one hour in the fridge.
20. Sprinkle with sea salt or a drizzle of dulce de leche or fabulous fruit.
21. Serve at room temperature to get all the FLAAAAAVOURS!!!

Breakfast Bagel Baps (Mockey-Ahh)**

INGREDIENTS
(MAKES 4)
160g Self Raising flour **See note for Gluten free
230g Greek Yoghurt....NOT Natural (I've tried and it's too sticky!) ** See note
1 egg (just for egg wash)
Sesame seeds or poppy seeds or Italian herbs ** See note

*NOTE

I just kept it simple and plain for my kids to eat and slowly introducing different flavours and toppings. Once you have the core recipe, feel free to go wild!

*I have tried it with natural yoghurt and the mix was too sloppy and sticky, but I have tried it with sour cream and it worked perfectly.

* I have dropped the quantity of sour cream to 200g and upped the flour to 180g! There is a difference too in brands of yoghurt.

Sour cream gives it a more scone taste and the yoghurt gives it a more chewy tinned croissant kinda taste but I'm still experimenting! #burp

* If you want to use plain flour, just add one teaspoon of baking powder. I tried two but felt although they rose well, there was a chemical aftertaste.

*I haven't made these gluten free yet but I think by changing the flour to Dove Gluten free and adding ¼ teaspoon of Xanthan gum and maybe a full egg or even egg white would help with the binding as the wetter the batter the better for gluten so feel free to experiment. I am still experimenting, but excited of the never ending possibilities!

Add dried herbs to the flour before you mix... add rosemary... add spices.. sun dried tomatoes... olives. Cinnamon and raisins... squeal, the excitement!

I would also add maybe another 5 or ten minutes to the baking time for gluten free because it would be a wetter dough, just keep an eye on them.

METHOD

1. Preheat the oven to 200C/400F/Gas 6.
2. Line the baking tray with non stick parchment. You'll thank me later!
3. Place the flour, baking powder in a bowl and gentle mix with your hands.
4. Dollop in the greek yoghurt and mix with a fork until it comes together in clumps.
5. In goes your hand like a claw and give it a few kneads until you have a lovely soft dough, only takes about a minute. I swear you will have the bagels made before the kettle boils!
6. Divide the dough into four portions.
7. Roll each portion into a ball and then into a long sausage and then wrap into a circle and overlap the join by sticking with a tiny bit of egg wash.
8. Use parchment paper or non stick mat or these will break your heart as they will stick to the tray.
9. Place the bagels spaced apart on the baking tray as these expand too while they bake so make sure they have loads of wiggle room to bake.
10. Don't panic if the dough is sticky, just add more flour and vice versa. if its too dry just add more yoghurt... just like goldilocks until you get it just right!
11. Glaze with egg wash before sprinkling with poppy seeds/sesame seeds or play around with what you have in your cupboard and bake in a hot preheated oven for 20 minutes.

N.B: LEAVE THEM COOL FOR 15 MINUTES BEFORE CUTTING.

**Mockey-ahhh spelled as pronounced means not real ... Irish slang! lol

Breakfast Filo Cups & Spicy Wedges

INGREDIENTS

6 eggs (or double up ingredients for 12!)
375g Filo pastry
(Defrosted about 3 sheets)
50g vintage cheddar cheese
1 teaspoon ted or/green/chilli jam/ onion marmalade/relish flavour of choice!
Crumbled feta cheese
Chopped spinach leaves
Parma ham
Finely slice spring onion
1 tablespoon butter
Salt (seasoning) and pepper (seasoning)

WEDGES

1½ teaspoons paprika
1 teaspoon garlic powder
½ teaspoon onion granules
½ teaspoon salt
½ teaspoon pepper
1 teaspoon sunflower oil
300g baby Potatoes cut into wedges

METHOD

1. Pre-heat the oven to 180C/350F/Gas 4.
2. Put the cut potato wedges into a large bowl and toss with 1 teaspoon of sunflower oil.
3. Sprinkle all the spices and seasoning into a small bowl and mix well. You can control the amount of seasoning, or like me throw it all in on top of the potato wedges and mix well.
4. Place skin side down so you have the spine of the potato on the tray and the exposed sides ready to crunch up in the oven. Bake for 40 minutes until golden brown and crispy.
5. Ten minutes before the potatoes are ready, crack on with the breakfast cups.
6. Grease a 6 cavity cupcake tray with melted butter or 12 if you want to double ingredients!
7. Unroll the pastry sheet from it's box and you should have 6-7 sheets.
8. Cut each filo sheet in half and then each half into quarters. So each sheet will yield 8 pieces. 4 sheets used for each breakfast cup. Make sure you always cover the filo as you work to prevent the pastry from drying out.
9. Brush 4 quarter sheets with melted butter and snuggle each piece into the cupcake tray, overlapping each piece and pressing against the side of the tray to create a filo pastry mould.
10. Pierce the base of each filo cup with a fork to let air circulate and prevent a soggy bottom, I brush the inside also with little pesto or relish or whatever you wish and then start layering the flaaaaaavours! Raid the fridge and see what you can come up with, such a versatile recipe.
11. I added tiny bite size pieces of chopped tomato, a sprinkling of vintage cheddar cheese, a twist of soft Parma ham, parsley and a pinch of black pepper. Splash of sriracha hot sauce just before serving gives a fab kick! Bake in the oven for 12 minutes for a wibble wobble egg or 15 minutes for a firmer egg.
12. Get creative with fillings… Finely chopped spinach leaves, crumbled feta cheese, parma ham … caramelised onion and garlic…Kids can make their own maybe with cooked ham or chicken, cheese and sweetcorn or chorizo, mozzarella and tomato paste … the list is endless!

Chocolate Chip Soda Bread

INGREDIENTS

450g Plain Flour
1 teaspoon Bicarbonate of soda
100g Caster sugar
100g Butter
350ml-400ml Buttermilk (May not need all of it)
1 large egg
150g Dark chocolate chips 55%
Grated rind of one orange (Optional)

METHOD

1. Pre heat the oven to 180C/350F/Gas4.
2. Add the flour, bicarbonate of soda, orange zest (if using) and butter into a bowl and blend together with your finger tips, gently squeezing the butter through your fingers with the flour until it resembles breadcrumbs. The blending technique using your finger tips is similar to dealing a pack of cards or "Show me the money".
3. Now add the sugar and chocolate chips and mix with your hand.
4. Make a well in the centre and crack in an egg. Now pour the milk (not all of it) around the bowl and reserve about 50mls as you may not need all the liquid depending on the size of the egg.
5. Make a claw shape with the hand and blend the dough, not too rough, just enough so the dough binds together, you want a soft not too wet dough, too wet and the dough will spread while baking.
6. On a lightly floured surface, knead lightly the dough into a round. Think of fairy wings and delicate butterflies as you knead the dough, you need to have a light touch!! Not Miss piggy wallops!
7. Place on a baking tray sprinkled with flour and bake for 40 minutes.

Trish's Top Tip

Soak 200g sultanas or raisins in orange juice overnight and this will plump up the fruit. Then add to the soda bread.
Cranberry and white chocolate is another lovely combination. Add 100g cranberries to the mix along with 100g white chocolate, reduce the caster sugar to 50g.
To make lime and coconut soda bread, add the zest of two limes and 50g coconut, reduce the flour to 400g.
Dried apricots are lovely too with the dark chocolate nibs. Reduce chocolate to 100g and add 100g chopped apricots (soaked juice of one orange overnight for extra bite).

Absolutely Divine!

No-Bake- Chocolate Ganache Tart

INGREDIENTS
250g Digestive biscuits
90g melted butter

GANACHE FILLING
300g 55% Dark chocolate chips
60g Butter
250ml Cream
30g Honey or brown sugar
1 teaspoon vanilla extract or rum!!!!
1 teaspoon coffee granules (optional)

METHOD

1. Melt the butter and whizz the digestives biscuits in a food processor or put them in a freezer bag and bash the living daylights out of them!
2. In a large bowl blend the melted butter and blitzed biscuits and then firmly press into a 9" loose bottom tin. Compress the mixture so it sets firmly, otherwise it will crumble when you try and cut a slice!
3. Leave to chill in the fridge for about 20-30 minutes until set.
4. While you're waiting, put the cream, chocolate, butter, sugar, vanilla extract and coffee granules (OPTIONAL) into a bowl, large enough so it can fit into a simmering pot of boiling water.
5. Make sure the base doesn't touch the water as you want the mixture to slowly melt and the chocolate to keep its delicious shine.
6. Once you have the 'chocolate soup' blended and deliciously smooth, just pour into the prepared biscuit shell!
7. Leave overnight chilled in the fridge before you face palm into the tart for breakfast!
8. Decorate if you wish with fresh fruit, or whipped cream or just a simple sprinkle of cocoa powder.
9. Ka-Boom you're done!

Easy peasy chockywockydoodah Day!

Cinnamon Rolls

INGREDIENTS
(MAKES 12)

475g Strong flour (or 450g depending on the size of the eggs)
1 Sachet of yeast (7g)
180ml Warm milk (not hot, not cold)
50g Sugar
1 Full egg (Large)
1 Egg yolk only (from a large egg)
50g very soft butter

FILLING

100g Brown Sugar
1 ½ tablespoons Cinnamon
60g very soft butter (soft enough to spread)

ICING

500g Icing sugar
2-3 tablespoons water (or more depends on how thick you want the icing)

METHOD

1. Pre heat the oven to 180C/350F/Gas4.
2. Line tray with parchment paper to prevent sticking (9 x 11 inch).
3. Attach the dough hook to the mixer and add flour, sprinkle the yeast on top and blend.
4. Warm the milk in the microwave for about 30 seconds to warm gently (Blood temperature).
5. Add the eggs to the milk and the sugar.
6. Turn on the mixer now add the egg mix to the flour and yeast, followed by the soft butter and blend for about 5 minutes until you have a lovely soft dough.
7. Transfer the dough to an oiled bowl and cover with a clean tea-towel and leave rest for about an hour or until double in size.
8. Once proved, deflate the dough by punching out the air, don't go full on karate kid, just enough to deflate the dough.
9. Roll out the dough to a rectangle about 11 x 13 inches.
10. Mix the brown sugar and cinnamon spice together until completely mixed through.
11. Smear the softened butter all over the dough and sprinkle with the sugar mix.
12. Use the tips of your fingers to spread evenly across the dough.
13. Give your hands a quick wash as you'll have cinnamon all over your fingers and you need them clean as you roll up your dough.
14. Starting from the far end roll the dough towards you using your fingers like a typewriter and moving across the dough as you roll up, like piano fingers, lol.
15. Once you have the sausage of dough rolled up, cut in half, then in quarters. Each quarter will yield three cinnamon rolls so you'll have 12 in total.
16. Fit them in a baking tray quite close together and let them prove again for another hour or two before they are baked.
17. Cover with slightly oiled cling film and let them snooze on the tray for about an hour to an hour and a half depending on how warm or cool the kitchen is.
18. At this stage you can also (once covered with clingfilm) put immediately in the fridge overnight to slowly prove . (Must give them an 1 hour or 1 ½ hours out of the fridge before you bake them off).
19. Bake for 20 minutes at 180C. Rotate after ten minutes. You want a golden glow rather than brown, too brown and the crust will be hard and the buns won't have the soft springy texture.
20. Once baked leave to cool for about 5 minutes before spreading the icing on top or it will start to melt before setting. (Glacé icing, mix icing sugar and enough water to create a paste).
21. Once cool, tear away and devour!

Baked Sugar Doughnuts

INGREDIENTS
(MAKES 12)

STEP 1
120g Strong White flour
40g Melted butter (salted)
50g caster sugar
1 sachets yeast (7g)
150ml lukewarm milk
2 egg yolks (Not the whites)
½ teaspoon vanilla extract

STEP 2
200g Strong white flour

GLAZE
1 tablespoon melted butter
50g caster sugar for dusting
½ teaspoon cinnamon (Optional)

METHOD

STEP 1
1. Pre-heat the oven to 180C/350C/Gas4.
2. Weigh out 120g of the strong white flour into a separate bowl (200g of flour will be left behind, it will be added in step 2).
3. Add 50g sugar to the 120g flour mix.
4. Then add the sachet of yeast to the sugar and flour mix.
5. Warm the milk in the microwave for about 30 seconds.
6. Melt 40g butter in the microwave (about 40 seconds until melted).
7. Add the melted butter to the milk and then add two egg yolks and mix until blended.
8. Pour the butter milk mixture over the flour, sugar, yeast mix and blend.
9. Cover the wet batter mixture with clingfilm and leave for ten minutes for the yeast to do its magic.

STEP 2
10. Once the timer has ding-a-linged now its time to slowly add the remaining (200g) flour, adding just enough until the dough holds together and no longer sticks to the bowl. Knead in the bowl for a few minutes, cover with lightly oiled cling film and rest for 45 minutes or until doubled in size.
11. Turn out the dough onto a floured board and roll out to about 1/2" thick, like a flat scone!
12. Cut out using a 2.5 inch cutter, keep dipping cutter into some flour as the dough is quite soft. Cut out 12 discs.
13. Cover with clingfilm and allow to prove until double in size about 30 minutes. I know it's a waiting game but sooooooo... worth the wait!
14. Bake for 10 minutes or until golden on top.
15. Once baked, let cool on a cooling rack for just a few minutes. While the doughnuts are still warm, brush each one with melted butter and roll into a bowl of sugar to lightly coat.
16. These doughnuts are best eaten on the day they are baked. Once they are cold they do lose their va-va-voom! So zap in microwave for ten seconds to revamp and you have yourself a delicious springy doughnut absolutely delicious in every way. Just perfect.

So Worth the Wait!...

Focaccia Bread (Overnight)

INGREDIENTS

570g Strong Bread Flour
10g Salt
1 Sachet of yeast (7g)
455g warm water
(Body temp, not hot not cold, luke warm)
4 tablespoons Olive oil
Maldon sea salt

METHOD

1. Preheat oven to 200C/400F Gas 6.
2. In a large bowl blend the flour, yeast and salt.
3. Next add the water, blend until the liquid is completely absorbed. Now don't panic as it will look very shaggy in appearance.
4. Rub the surface of the dough lightly with some olive oil, cover with a damp cloth and leave in the fridge overnight or at least 12 hours. It will double and explode in size overnight!
5. The beauty of this bread is that you can mix it at night and take it out in the morning and have it baked and ready for lunch!
6. Grease a tray with olive oil. I used a large baking tray 11 x 14 but you can also split the dough in two and use two 9" sandwich tins or a roasting tray.
7. Pour a tablespoon of oil into the centre of the pan. Take the chilled Focaccia dough out of the fridge and next grease your hands with olive oil.
8. Using your fingertips release the dough from the sides of the bowl and pulling it towards the centre, rotating the bowl as you deflate the dough.
9. Next pull the dough from 12 O'Clock to 6 O'Clock and turn the bowl in quarters as you stretch the dough.
10. Place in the prepared oiled tray. Pour a tablespoon of olive oil over the dough and let it rest at room temperature for about 3 hours depending on the temperature of the kitchen.
11. Once proved, rub your hands with oil and using your fingertips press straight down to create deep dimples/ Gently stretch the dough as you dimple to allow the dough to fill the tray.
12. Sprinkle with sea salt all over.
13. Transfer to the oven and bake for 25 minutes to 30 minutes until golden and crisp.
14. Transfer baked Focaccia to a rack to cool, leave to cool for 10 minutes before cutting.

Trish's Top Tip

Use chopped rosemary and garlic or caramelised onions. Get creative with toppings. My kids love the uncomplicated salt addition but I love rosemary garlic and thyme! Go wild!

Go Wild!

French Fruit Galette

INGREDIENTS

1x 375g packet of Puff pastry ** Or GF Pastry
100g Brown sugar (Caster or granulated is fine too)
2 heaped tablespoons cornflour (If using fresh reduce to one)
250g Frozen mixed berries (200g fresh berries if using)
1 squeeze of lemon juice (optional)
1 Egg (for glaze) ** OR Soy milk if dairy free
Sugar nibs for sprinkling (optional)
Icing sugar (for dusting)
2 tablespoons of Raspberry Jam
2 tablespoons ground almonds

METHOD

1. Pre-heat the oven to 200C/400F/Gas 6.
2. Unroll the puff pastry (It takes about 15 minutes at room temperature for it too be pliable enough to unroll).
3. Put the pastry back in the fridge to chill for 20 minutes.
4. Once you're ready to start and have all the ingredients ready and weighed, take the pastry out of the fridge.
5. In a bowl mix the berries, cornflour and sugar along with a squeeze of lemon.
6. Prick the base of the pastry just where you're going to pile the fruit.
7. Smear the area now with the raspberry jam as this creates a barrier between the fruit and the pastry and you won't end up with a soggy bottom!
8. Sprinkle the ground almonds on top of the raspberry jam again to create an additional barrier for soakage.
9. Pile the frozen fruit in the middle of the pastry and pile high like a mountain of deliciousness!!!!
10. Start folding the edges of the pastry up and over the edge of the fruit so you contain all the fruit like a cage and brush the edges generously with the egg wash.
11. Sprinkle with some sugar nibs.
12. Drop the temperature to 180C/350F/Gas 4 just before you put the pastry into the oven.
13. Bake for 30 minutes until golden brown of longer. You need to have the pastry golden brown to make sure the pastry is well cooked. The cornflour thickens the fruit (once you see it bubbling in the oven).
14. Once done remove from the oven and let the pastry sit for at least 30 minutes... set a timer if you have to! Do not eat it or you'll end up with a burned gob and an unnecessary trip to A&E!!
15. Dust with some icing sugar before serving and a good dollop of ice-cream...

Trish's Top Tip

**For Gluten free all you need is to change the pastry to GF Pastry and the same for Dairy Free. Use almond or soy milk for glazing. Be careful too of what jam you use!
Pearl sugar, also called nib sugar, is a type of specialty sugar that will not dissolve into baked goods.

Yum...Yum... Diddle Dee... Dum...get some in ma belly!!!!

Hot Cross Buns

INGREDIENTS

100g Caster Sugar
550g Plain Strong Flour
1 sachet of yeast (7g sachet)
75g Light brown sugar
300ml milk (warmed to hand temperature)
50g Softened butter
1 small egg
75g Sultanas (I like to soak mine in orange juice overnight)
50g mixed peel or chopped apricot (optional)
Zest orange
1 teaspoon cinnamon
½ teaspoon mixed spice

CROSS BATTER

75g flour
5 tablespoons water

METHOD

1. Pre heat the oven to 180C/350F/Gas 4 and grease the tray.
2. Put the flour, yeast, sugar and spices into a bowl.
3. Drop the butter into the warmed milk to dissolve.
4. Add the milk mix to the flour mix and blend, you can do this by hand but a mixer with a dough hook attached will save your sanity. Make yourself a cup of tea and wait for about 5 minutes for the dough to come together.
5. You will have a sticky dough, don't panic.
6. At this stage scrape the dough out of the bowl and place on a floured board.
7. Add fruit to the dough and knead for another couple of minutes until completely mixed through.
8. Roll the dough out into a sausage shape and cut into 12 portions.
9. Each portion is approximately 100g, it helps to weigh them so they are all the same size.
10. Roll each piece into a round ball and place on a greased tray.
11. Cover clingfilm with some oil and place over the dough like a blanket and let the dough balls snooze and rest for about 40 minutes to an hour until they are doubled in size.
12. Prepare the cross batter by blending the flour and water and then putting into a piping bag.
13. Pipe a thin line from the top of the bun all the way to the bottom of the tray, turn the tray and repeat so you have a criss cross pattern across the buns.
14. Bake for 20 minutes.
15. Once golden brown take out of the oven and place a rack to cool.
16. Glaze with some apricot jam and devour!

43

Irish Soda Bread

INGREDIENTS
300g Plain White flour
300g Brown Flour
1tsp salt
1tsp Bicarbonate of soda
420ml Buttermilk milk
Magic dust (optional!)

METHOD

1. Preheat the oven to 200C/400F/Gas 6.
2. Grease baking tray.
3. Mix together the flours, salt and bicarbonate of soda.
4. Add milk and mix to a soft dough.
5. Turn onto a lightly floured surface and knead for about a minute to give a smooth dough.
6. Shape into a round shape and make a cross with a knife to let the fairies out!!
7. Place on a floured tray.
8. Bake for 35-40 minutes until golden brown and well risen.
9. Cool and devour!

Trish's Top Tip

If you can't get buttermilk, just add two teaspoons of lemon juice to the milk and let it sit for 5 or 10 minutes to let it do its magic…. Or add vinegar for the same effect.

Enjoy… #micdrop

2 Minute No Yeast Naan Bread

INGREDIENTS
(SERVES 4)
100g Self raising flour
¼ teaspoon salt
100g natural Yoghurt
½ teaspoon dried Rosemary or Thyme (optional)

METHOD

1. Put all the dry ingredients into a mixing bowl, including the herbs (if using).
2. Now add the yoghurt and stir until well combined.
3. Knead into a little flour ball and cover for 10 or 15 minutes to settle.
4. Cut into four and finely roll our each dough piece into a flattened Naan.
5. Place on a pre-heated frying pan (no oil) and dry fry until you see little bubble air pockets forming.
6. Flip over and cook for another minute.
7. I like to have a pot of warm water simmering away with a bowl and plate ready to place my naan bread in to keep warm before I serve.
8. I don't microwave as you lose the soft pillowy texture.
9. Brush with some melted flavoured butter of choice and chopped parsley

Trish's Top Tip

Sauté an onion or clove of garlic (or both) until caramelised, cool and add to dry flour mix.

Or...

Add a little chilli flakes to spice up the Naan.
Add some sweetness by replacing the salt with ½ teaspoon of caster sugar and adding ¼ teaspoon cinnamon. Serve with natural yoghurt and some fresh berries with a drizzle honey.
Use as a wrap and fill with your favourite lunch fillings.
Crack an egg on top and serve with bacon for breakfast ......

Na -Na -Na -Na- Na- Na- Na -Na…….NAAN BREAD

Pizza Dough

INGREDIENTS

500g Strong plain flour
1 sachet of dried yeast
300ml warm water (Body temperature)
1 tsp salt
1 tablespoon olive oil

METHOD

1. Preheat oven to 200C/400F/Gas 6.
2. In a bowl place the flour and dried yeast and mix.
3. Using a jug, measure out 300ml of warm water and add a teaspoon of salt, and stir so the salt dissolves.
4. Add one tablespoon of olive oil to the flour mix and pour in all the water and stir with your hand.
5. It will be sticky but will feel warm to the touch or you can use your stand alone mixer with a dough hook attached or use your hand like a mixer and keep bringing it all together.
6. Tip the ball of dough onto a floured worktop and knead up and down and turn it around, 12 O'Clock to 6 O'Clock and turn it around!
7. This will take about 5 minutes in mixer or longer by hand (about 7 minutes) but it's a lovely way to feel how the pizza dough is doing.
8. Once kneaded, leave in an oiled bowl and cover with a tea-towel. A little oil wiped into the bowl stops the mix from sticking.
9. Leave to proof for about 15 minutes (for larger amounts could be 30 minutes).
10. While you are waiting, pre-heat the oven to 200C/400F/Gas 6.
11. These bake in about 15 minutes or less. Keep an eye on them as they cook fast depending on the oven.
12. Shape the pizza into whatever shape you would like, Pizza Pinwheels or Octo-pizza or just pizza. The main thing is to have fun baking!
13. Using passata sauce/tomato sauce smear some on the pizza in a swirl using a spoon and bring right to the edges. Sprinkle with mozzarella cheese and topping of your choice or make some fun faces using pepperoni, sliced chorizo and olives.
14. Roll up dough if creating the pinwheels and cut into rings like sushi rolls ... or split dough into two, one piece is the octopus body and the rest are tentacles...made into bread sticks for dipping!

Pop Tarts

INGREDIENTS
180g Plain flour
100g Cold butter (cubed into small pieces)
1 tablespoon of sugar
1 Egg yolk
2 tablespoons of cold water

ICING
1 Egg white
200g /250g Icing sugar

METHOD

1. Place the flour and cold butter into a bowl.
2. Using your fingers, break up the butter into the flour until it looks like breadcrumbs... using your "Show me the money" technique.
3. Now add the tablespoon of sugar and mix through.
4. Once all the butter is blended into the flour, make a well in the centre of the bowl and add the egg yolk.
5. Carefully add cold water around the mixture like a swirl so it gets mixed in properly and doesn't clump.
6. Now using a butter knife, start blending the mixture in a criss cross motion so it brings the pastry together. Using a knife helps break up the flour mixture and prevents the butter from melting and getting too warm from your hands.
7. Once the pastry is nearly all combined, use your hand like a claw and gently pull the pastry together.
8. Once the dough comes together, shape into a ball and then flatten so it chills faster in the fridge. Cover with clingfilm and let it snooze for about 10 minutes or you can roll it out straight away.
9. Sprinkle the worktop with some flour... not too much as you don't want to dry out the pastry, then begin to roll out the pastry.
10. Try and keep it in a rectangle shape as it makes it easier to cut.
11. Keep in mind you need to roll it out thinly as you will be sandwiching each panel together to form the pop tart.
12. Once rolled out, cut into rectangle shapes about four finger width, you will get 12 panels out of the pastry.
13. Put a generous teaspoon of jam in the middle of one pop tart making sure you are a finger away from the edge so the jam doesn't spill out.
14. Brush the edge of the pop tart with egg wash and then carefully lift the top of the pop tart and snuggle around the jam. It now looks like a giant ravioli. They can be sandwiched with the jam panel and sealed tight.
15. Press a fork over the sandwiched pastry to crimp the edges. Leave to chill in the fridge for 20 minutes while you preheat the oven.
16. Line the tray with parchment paper and place in a preheated oven at 180C for 15-20 minutes until golden. Leave the pop tarts cool before you add the icing.

ICING

17. Sift the icing sugar into a bowl and add egg white until the icing becomes thick enough to coat the back of a spoon. If necessary add more water (a drop at a time) or icing sugar to adjust consistency. You can also add a drop or two of colour if you want a splash of hot pink! Cover with sprinkles and leave to set. Once dry... enjoy with a delicious hot cuppa something!

Enjoy with a delicious hot cuppa something!

Potato & Blue Cheese Savoury Tart

INGREDIENTS
(MAKES 12)

320g Jus-Rol Block of pastry (or whatever shop brand you prefer)
150g Gorgonzola Picante cheese
60g Mascarpone cheese
3 tablespoons cream (50ml)
2 large potatoes (thinly sliced, I used red rooster)
2 tablespoons Olive oil (for the potato)
1 red onion (thinly sliced)
Black pepper
Salt
1 egg yolk (egg wash)
1 tablespoon milk (egg wash)
Fresh Rosemary (Optional)

METHOD

1. Preheat the oven to 200C/400F/Gas 6.
2. Take the pastry out of the fridge 20 minutes before you need to use it (easier to unroll).
3. Unroll the pastry and place on a greased tray lined with baking parchment.
4. Chill pastry while you slice the potatoes and onions. No point in leaving it hanging around while you chop!
5. Toss the sliced potatoes with the oil and mix well, the oil helps cook the potatoes in the oven.
6. Using a knife score about an inch away from the edge to create a border all the way around the puff pastry.
7. With a fork, prick the base within the rectangle but not at the border. Remember you want the border to rise.

DO NOT PRICK THE BORDER OR THE PASTRY WILL DEFLATE WHILE BAKING.

8. You want the walls of the puff pastry to rise while the potato and cheese filling bubbles away and are contained within the border.
9. Next mix the cream and mascarpone along with most of the gorgonzola to a paté and spread the base of the pastry tart (within the walls of the border) This acts as a barrier and prevents the pastry from getting soggy.
10. Sprinkle the rest of the gorgonzola on the cheese base, scatter the onion over the cheese mixture and layer thinly sliced potato on top of the onion.
11. At this stage you could also add a touch of chopped rosemary to the mix for another Flaaaaaaavour ....
12. Season with a little sea salt and ground black pepper.
13. Place in the oven for 25 minutes until golden and bubbling.
14. Remove and cool on a rack before slicing and serving with a gorgeous salad and cold glass of something.

Ka-BOOM!

Porridge Bread

INGREDIENTS
(SERVES 10 SLICES)

400g Porridge Oats
2 teaspoons Bicarbonate of soda
1 teaspoon salt
1 x 500ml pot Natural Yoghurt
1 egg (Large)
Sprinkle of pumpkin seeds
(optional)

METHOD

1. Preheat the oven to 200C/400F/Gas 6.
2. Grease a 2lb loaf tin (900g).
3. Place the oats into a bowl along with the salt and bicarbonate of soda, mix together until blended.
4. Crack an egg into the mix.
5. Pour the yoghurt on top of the oat mix and stir gently.
6. At this stage you could also add a tablespoon of seeds for added crunch.
7. Line the base of the tin with greaseproof paper to prevent it sticking then dollop the mixture into the tin.
8. Sprinkle the top with seeds (optional).
9. Bake for 40/45minutes.
10. Once baked leave the bread sit in the tin before removing it.
11. Run a knife around the tin to loosen and tip the bread out on to a cooling rack.
12. The bread should have a hollow sound when tapped.
13. If undecided put back in the oven for another 5 minutes upside down so the base is exposed to the oven heat and it will certainly have cooked by the time the kettle is boiled!

Pop on the Kettle!

Twisted Pretzels

INGREDIENTS
650g Strong Flour
1 teaspoon salt
1 tablespoon Caster Sugar
350ml lukewarm water
60g salted butter (melted)
1 Sachet dried yeast (7g)

MAGIC PRETZEL BATH WATER
2.2litres of water
120g Bread soda

GLAZE
1 Egg (glaze)
1 tablespoons coarse sea salt (I love Maldon course sea flakes)

METHOD

1. Pre-heat the oven to 200C/400F/Gas 6.
2. Add the teaspoon of salt to the warm water and pour into the mixer. Attach the dough hook if using. Sprinkle in the sugar and stir, followed by the sachet of dried yeast sprinkled on top.
3. Leave for about 4-5 minutes so the yeast as time to kick start and foam a little.
4. Once you have the slight foam from the yeast mix, throw in all the flour followed by the melted butter and turn on the mixer.
5. Let the machine do all the handwork so you don't have to. It takes about 5 minutes in my Kenwood.
6. The dough will start to come away from the sides of the mixer and gather into a smooth dough. (Grease your hands a little as this will help slide the dough off the hook when removing).
7. Knead the dough for just a minute into a dough ball, oil the bowl and put the dough back to rest for about 40 minutes to an hour, just until it has nearly doubled in size.
8. While waiting, prepare the pretzel bath…
9. Fill a pot with 2.2 litres of water and add 120g bread soda and bring to a boil, once boiling turn the heat down and let simmer until ready to dunk the pretzels.
10. It's important to give the pretzels a warm soda bath as this will give the signature shiny coat, chewiness and texture to them. Don't skip this part!!!
11. Once the dough has proved, tip onto a floured worktop and divide into 8 for large pretzels or 16 for smaller ones.
12. Roll each piece into a long sausage almost the length of your arm. Shape the sausage into a "U" and then fold left over right and right over left for the signature twist or get creative…
13. Dip each pretzel into the hot soda bath for twenty seconds, no more or the pretzels can have a metallic aftertaste. Scoop out using a slotted spoon and gently place on the parchment paper or silicone mat. Glaze with a little egg and sprinkle generously with coarse sea salt.
14. Bake in a pre-heated oven for 15-20 minutes depending on the size you make the pretzel.
15. Once baked, let cool for 15 minutes and enjoy with a variety of dips and dunks or slather with cream cheese. Split the pretzel horizontally and fill with ham etc… or whatever tickles your tastebuds!

Profiteroles

INGREDIENTS
65g Plain or strong flour
50g Butter
2 large eggs
150ml water

CHOCOLATE SAUCE
125g Plain dark chocolate (55%)
15g Butter
30ml golden syrup
2 tablespoons milk (optional)
½ teaspoon vanilla extract (optional)

FILLING
150ml Double cream

METHOD

1. Pre heat the oven to 180C/350F/Gas 4.
2. Sieve the flour onto a piece of paper, this makes it easier to slide into the pot when making the choux.
3. Put the butter and water in a saucepan and heat gently until the butter has melted, then bring to a rapid boil. Remove the pan from the heat and immediately tip in the flour.
4. Beat thoroughly with a wooden spoon, continue beating over a low heat until the mixture forms a ball in the centre of the pan. Make sure you don't overheat as you don't want the mixture to become fatty.
5. Remove from the heat and cool for a minute or two as you don't want to end up with scrambled egg when you mix the egg mixture through the hot choux paste.
6. This is where I hand it over to my work colleague "Ken" Wood. My mixer loves to beat the living daylights out of things so I don't have to or you can use a wooden spoon and tone up those upper arms.
7. Beat in the eggs a little at a time adding only just enough to give a piping consistency.
8. It's important to incorporate as much air as possible. It should have a plopping consistency.
9. Put the choux paste into a pastry bag with or without a nozzle and pipe about 20 small choux buns on a non stick baking sheet or spoon the mixture into small rounds.
10. Bake at 180C for 20-25 minutes until they are golden brown. Keep an eye on them though as the size of the choux buns that will dictate the baking time.
11. I like to stab each bun and make a hole in the side to release any steam and I don't want any soggy bottoms, as they say nobody likes a soggy bottom!
12. While you start the open bun surgery, reduce the oven temp to 160C and then once slit pop them back in the oven for about 5 minutes to dry out completely.
13. Leave to cool on a wire rack.

CHOCOLATE SAUCE

14. For the chocolate sauce, melt the chocolate, butter and golden syrup in a small saucepan over a very low heat and stir until smooth. You can add ½ teaspoon of vanilla extract if you wish, and for a thinner coat of chocolate add 2 tablespoons of milk to the chocolate soup!
15. Whip the cream until it just holds shape. Spoon the cream into a piping bag and use to fill each little choux bun with cream through the holes you've created. Pour with cream and pour chocolate sauce over the top and KA-BOOM you've created the profiterole masterpiece!

Trish's Top Tip

Oiling a spoon or dipping in boiling water helps the syrup glide off when measuring. If pouring directly from the rim, oil the rim!

Puff Pastry Cones

INGREDIENTS

320g Jus-Rol Puff Pastry sheet
12 Ice cream cones wrapped in foil as moulds (If using)
Or 12 paper cones wrapped with foil as moulds
1 egg (Beaten for egg wash)
1 teaspoons Poppy seeds (optional)
1 teaspoon Sesame Seeds (optional)
1 teaspoon Caster sugar (optional)
250ml Whipped cream
250g Strawberries

METHOD

1. Pre-heat the oven to 200C /400F/Gas 6.
2. As you wait for the oven to heat up, take the pastry out of the fridge 20 minutes before you want to use it.
3. Unroll the puff pastry and cut into strips down the longest side.
4. Grease the pastry cones, or if you don't have metal pastry cones, you can easily make your own using foil and A4 paper or you can tightly wrap ice cream cones with foil too. Get inventive!
5. Starting at the pointed end, wrap a pastry strip around the mould in a spiral, with each line overlapping slightly. Repeat to cover all the moulds.
6. Brush the pastry all over with the beaten egg and sprinkle with granulated sugar or sesame seeds or poppy seeds for added crunch.
7. Place the horns on their sides on a non-stick baking tray and put into the oven for 12- 15 minutes or until the cones are golden-brown and crisp.
8. Transfer to a wire rack to cool completely. Once cool, carefully remove the moulds (using a clean tea towel to help you). Hold the cone in one hand and gently twist with the other and the pastry cone just pops off. Be gentle as the pastry is still very fragile until it cools.
9. This is where the fun begins, make them either sweet or savoury, suggestions....

Puff Pastry Cone Continued ->

SWEET FILLING:

1. Spread Nutella in the inside shell before adding some chopped strawberries and piped whipped cream, sprinkled with some shaved chocolate.
2. Dip the cones in melted dark chocolate before you fill with chopped fresh fruit or custard cream. Much easier to pipe the cream instead of spooning into the cone, so place the whipped cream into a piping bag fitted with star nozzle and then pipe the mixture into the pastry cones. Top with some more fruit and serve immediately.

SAVORY FILLING:

3. Spread mustard, or horseradish or pesto or chilli jam etc in the inside shell and add chopped ham, chopped chicken, chopped spring onion, torn lettuce, cheese or whatever you fancy.

Trish's Top Tip

To make your own horn moulds, use two A4 sheets of paper one on top of the other (this gives the cone strength and stability).
Sit the pieces of paper on top of an oblong piece of foil (about an inch bigger than the A4 sheets). Starting from the right hand bottom corner, twist and rotate the paper first from right to left and it automatically twists into a cone shape. Secure with tape, repeat with the piece of foil and wrap tightly around to create the cone.
Grease very well to prevent pastry from sticking.
Buy remade ice-cream cones and wrap each one tightly with foil, for the same effect.

Quiche Lorraine

PASTRY INGREDIENTS
180g Plain Flour
100g Cold Butter (Salted)
1 egg yolk
2 or 3 tablespoon cold water (I used two)
Spring of fresh times leaves (Optional)

FILLING
250g cooked ham
3 Large Eggs
300ml Cream
80g Strong mature cheddar cheese

METHOD

1. Pre heat the oven to 180C/350F/Gas 4 and grease the 9" flan tin.
2. Put the flour and cold butter into a bowl and blend between you fingers. The method I use is "Show me the money". As you do, you flatten the butter into small pieces as it blends and disappears into the flour like breadcrumbs.
3. Add fresh thyme or if you want to add another layer of Flaaaaaaavour add some chilli flakes.
4. Make a well in the centre of the flour butter mix and add the egg yolk.
5. Sprinkle the cold water around the bowl and use a butter knife to blend in a criss cross pattern across the bowl to represent the mixing blade. I don't use my hand until I can see the pastry come together in clumps. The colour changes too as the butter is mixed and egg yolk to a pale yellow.
6. Now's the time to go in with your hand like a claw and mix the dough. Keep your hand stiff as you move around the bowl and the pastry will come together in a clump. You can start a gentle knead with your hand still in the bowl to bring the dough together.
7. Sprinkle some flour on the worktop and roll out you dough.
8. Now any normal person would let this pastry chill for 30 minutes but then again I'm not normal. Roll out the dough immediately to fit the round 9" flan tin. Using the rolling pin, roll up and down and move the pastry around, so up down and turn it around, so just think from 12 O'Clock to 6 O'Clock and twist the pastry each time so it doesn't stick on the worktop.
9. Use the rolling pin as a guide to roll the pastry back on to the rolling pin so you can lift in place and cover the tin. I use a 9" loose bottomed flan tin. Prick the pastry base with a fork on the base and along the sides.
10. Now you can chill the pastry for 30 minutes to an hour to settle so the pastry doesn't shrink when baked.
11. Bake the pastry case "blind" which means ... place some foil directly onto the flan tin to create a blanket of foil and weigh down with either ceramic beans or dry beans or even rice.
12. Bake for 15 minutes, then take out of the oven and remove the foil (be careful as the foil is hot and the beans are mobile!!!) and bake for another 5-8 minutes until the pastry is pale golden and cooked.
13. When the pastry case is completely cold, fill with the prepared filling.

FILLING

14. Whisk the egg and cream together.
15. Sprinkle cheese on the base followed by cooked ham and then pour the cream mixture on top.
16. Bake in the oven for 25 minutes until just set (it should have a slight wobble).
17. Take out and cool in tin.
18. The quiche will set with the residual heat in the tin so you don't want to over cook it.
19. Slice that baby up after 10 minutes cooling and devour with lovely side salad and maybe a glass of something cold!

Kids Sausage Rolls - Easy Peasy

INGREDIENTS
Jus-rol puff pastry roll (320g)
Pork Sausages of choice (454g)
1 egg (for egg wash)
Sesame seeds (optional)
Ketchup / BBQ / Chutney /
Onion marmalade (Optional)

METHOD

1. Preheat the oven 180C/350F/Gas 4.
2. Take the pastry out of the fridge 30 minutes before you need (it's easier to unroll).
3. Unfold the pastry and lay it out with the wide side facing you like a rectangle. Keep it on the paper it came on as it's easier to work with and less mess!
4. Take the sausages out of the packet and remove the skin on each one using a scissors or knife and carefully take the skin off the sausages (Adult supervision may be required).
5. Slice the sausage vertically down the middle of the sausage and the skin just peels off.
6. Keep the shape of the sausage as you're going to sit that on the pastry but don't worry it's squishy. You can mould it with your fingers into a sausage shape.
7. Using a pastry brush, take some egg wash and brush it across the width of the pastry or even brush a tasty sauce like ketchup or BBQ sauce to help stick the pastry and seal together once wrapped.
8. Line up a trail of sausages on the pastry head to toe.
9. Now fold the pastry towards you until completely wrapped and seal again with a little egg wash so you tuck the pastry under the sausages and the seal is hidden.
10. You should have a huge sausage roll ready to cut into bite sizes.
11. Using a knife or a pizza wheel, cut away the excess pastry and place on a tray with baking parchment to prevent sticking.
12. Chill in the fridge for 10 minutes before you cut them into shape. It makes them easier to cut.
13. Take them out of the fridge and cut them into three inch bite sizes or larger depending on how hungry you are!
14. Just remember to cut each sausage roll the same size so they bake evenly.
15. Brush again with a little beaten egg to glaze and if you like sprinkle with some sesame seeds.
16. Bake in the pre-heated oven for 20-25minutes (depends on how large you cut the rolls).
17. Bake until they are golden brown.
18. Leave to cool on rack for 10 minutes before you eat them as they are too hot to enjoy and may burn your mouth!!
19. BOOM!! Banging sausage rolls perfect for breakfast lunch or dinner!

BOOM! Banging sausage rolls

Granny's Guinness Treacle Bread

INGREDIENTS

454g Whole Wheat Brown Flour
30g Porridge Oats
2 teaspoons Bicarbonate of soda
60g Butter
30g Dark Brown Sugar
100g Treacle
330ml Guinness (Dark Stout)

METHOD

1. Pre-heat the oven to 190C/400F/Gas 6.
2. Grease a 2lb loaf tin.
3. Place the flour into a large bowl and add the bicarbonate of soda, brown sugar and mix well, making sure there are no lumps of sugar. Mash with a fork if necessary.
4. Next add the butter and blend using your fingertips into the flour mix until it resembles bread crumbs.
5. I slowly add some Guinness to my weighed out treacle to help loosen the sticky molasses from the container as it makes is much easier to pour. (oiling the lip of the treacle tin helps too if you want to pour directly from the can into the container).
6. Add in the treacle and Guinness mix until completely combined, with no visible lumps or bumps of flour.
7. Transfer to a greased 2lb loaf tin and bake for 45 minutes in a preheated oven.
8. You'll know when the loaf is baked as the base of the loaf will sound hollow.
9. Transfer to a cooking rack and wait 15 minutes before cutting.
10. Slather with some Irish butter or jam or both or whatever tickles your fancy!

Ka-Boom! You're done!

Twisted Milk Plait

INGREDIENTS
450g Strong White flour
15g butter
½ teaspoon salt
1 teaspoon of caster sugar
1 sachet yeast (7g)
290ml lukewarm milk
Glaze
1 egg lightly beaten

METHOD

1. Preheat the oven to 190C/375 F/Gas 5.
2. Grease and dust the 12 x 9 inch baking tray with flour.
3. Sieve together the flour, salt in a bowl and rub in the butter. Add yeast.
4. Now add the dry mix to the mixer with a dough attachment attached.
5. Dissolve the sugar in warmed milk and stir, now add the warmed milk to the dry ingredients and knead to a soft dough. It takes a few minutes.
6. Take the dough out of the mixer and roll into a long sausage shape.
7. Divide into three equal parts, using a scales if you need to and roll into three evenly shaped dough balls. Cover with lightly oiled cling film and allow it to rest for 5 minutes.
8. Roll each dough ball into a long sausage shape, until you have three long strips of dough.
9. Start the plait by laying one tip on top of the next tip of dough until you have a stack secured in place to start the plait.
10. Now cross over .. left over middle..right over middle.. left over middle ..until you reach the end and then using the heel of your hand flatten the dough to secure the end and same for the top and tuck underneath to hide.
11. Place on greased baking tray and cover with oiled clingfilm. Allow to prove until double in size, about 40 minutes.
12. Remove cling film, beat egg and glaze.
13. Bake for 25 to 30 minutes until golden brown and well risen.
14. Place on a wire rack and cool and devour!

Trish's Top Tip

Add some chopped sun-dried tomatoes/olives/nuts and herbs into the dry mix before blending for a savoury twist As a variation when glazing before baking sprinkle on some poppy seeds or sesame seeds.

Vegetarian Quiche

INGREDIENTS

180g Plain Flour
100g Cold Butter (Salted)
1 egg yolk
2 or 3 tablespoon cold water (I used two)
Spring of fresh times leaves (Optional)

FILLING

2 tablespoons olive oil
2 Red peppers sliced and diced (I used one yellow one red)
3 Garlic cloves (crushed)
1 Large Onion (sliced and diced)
4 Baby mushrooms (sliced and diced)
½ Courgette (large, sliced and quartered)
6 cherry tomatoes (sliced and diced)
4 Large Eggs (Beaten)
250ml cream
150g Feta cheese (crumbled)
1 teaspoon red pesto (Optional)

METHOD

1. Pre heat the oven to 180C/350F/Gas4 and grease the 9" flan tin.
2. Put the flour and cold butter into a bowl and blend between you fingers. The method I use is "Show me the money". Blend the butter and flour between your fingertips and as you do you flatten the butter into small pieces as it blends and disappears into the flour like breadcrumbs.
3. Add the fresh thyme if you want to add another layer of Flaaaaaaaavour or even chilli flakes.
4. Make a well in the centre of the flour butter mix and add the egg yolk.
5. Sprinkle the cold water around the bowl and use a butter knife to blend in a criss cross pattern across the bowl to represent the mixing blade. I don't use my hand until I can see the pastry come together in clumps, the colour changes too as the butter is mixed and egg yolk to a pale yellow.
6. Now's the time to go in with your hand like a claw and mix the dough, keep your hand stiff as you move around the bowl and the pastry will come together in a clump. You can start a gentle knead with your hand still in the bowl to bring the dough together.
7. Pastry done … Ka-Boom!
8. Sprinkle some flour on the worktop and roll out you dough.
9. Roll out the dough immediately to fit the round 9" flan tin, using the rolling pin, roll up and down and move the pastry around, so up down and turn it around, so just think from 12 O'Clock to 6 O'Clock and twist the pastry each time so it doesn't stick on the worktop.
10. Use the rolling pin as a guide to roll the pastry back on to the rolling pin so you can lift in place and cover the tin. I use a 9" loose bottomed flan tin. Prick the pastry base with a fork on the base and along the sides.
11. Now you can chill the pastry for 30 minutes to an hour to settle so the pastry doesn't shrink when baked.
12. Bake the pastry case "blind" which means … place some foil directly onto the flan tin to create a blanket of foil and weigh down with either ceramic beans or dry beans or even rice.
13. Bake for 15 minutes, then take out of the oven remove the foil (be careful as the foil is hot and the beans are mobile!!!) and bake for another 5-8 minutes until the pastry is pale golden and cooked.
14. When the pastry case is completely cold, fill with the prepared filling.

Vegetarian Quiche Continued ->

FILLING

15. Put two tablespoons of oil in the frying pan and sauté the chopped onion for a few minutes until translucent, followed by the crushed garlic.
16. Next throw in the peppers and the chopped courgette. Sauté again for 5 minutes on a low heat. Keep stirring to prevent burning.
17. Next add the chopped tomatoes and mushrooms and simmer on a low heat for 5 minutes, then turn off the heat and leave go completely cold. I normally make the ratatouille the night before so I have everything ready and at hand. This quiche then takes only minutes to prepare.
18. Whisk four eggs and add 250ml cream to the egg mix and lightly whisk so you have a smooth egg batter.
19. Get everything ready for the assembly line. Pastry case …. Ratatouille, feta cheese, egg and cream.
20. Transfer the pastry flan tin to a large baking tray to avoid spillage.
21. Fill the pastry case with the cold vegetable mix and spread out evenly. Scatter the feta cheese and slowly pour the egg cream batter into the shell and into the nooks and crannies of the vegetable base.
22. Bake in a preheated oven for 25 minutes. There should be a very little soft wobble left once baked. If still too wobbly put back in oven for a further 5 minutes but no longer.
23. A mini quiche quiche typically takes 10-15 minutes only but check after 10 minutes so they don't burn.
24. The quiche will set with the residual heat in the tin so you don't want to over cook it.
25. Slice that baby up after 10 minutes cooling and devour with lovely side salad and maybe a glass of something!

oh Pilates? I thought you said … Pie & Lattes.

WHAT DO YOU CALL STRAWBERRIES
PLAYING THE GUITAR?...
A JAM SESSION!

LOAF CAKES & TRADITIONAL BAKES

BAKING IS ALL ABOUT TAKING...WHISKS

Apple And Mixed Berry Crumble

INGREDIENTS

200g Bramley apples, peeled and chopped
200g Frozen mixed berries
150g Plain Flour
100g Cold salted butter
75g Dark Brown Sugar
50g Porridge oats
2 tablespoons of caster sugar (for mixed fruit)
9" Baking dish

METHOD

1. Pre heat the oven at 180C/350F/Gas 4.
2. Place flour in a bowl and add chopped cold butter.
3. Cut butter into small cubes to make it easier to blend with flour... technique... "show me the money".
4. Using your fingers, break up the butter and blend with the flour. Don't over mix as you want to have a few lumps of butter so they melt in the oven and give a lovely crust to the crumble.
5. Once flour and butter are mixed together, add the brown sugar and stir, then finally add the oats.
6. Empty the apples and mixed berries into the tin and spread out evenly.
7. Sprinkle two tablespoons of caster sugar on top of the fruit mix.
8. Now sprinkle the crumble mix on top of the fruit. Be sure to cover all the fruit and gently press down like fairy tip toes.
9. The crumble needs to be light and airy so make sure you gently pat the crumble. There is a lot of crumble but that shrinks down as the fruit is cooking so don't worry if it looks like a mountain!
10. Place the tin on a tray to prevent any fruit juice spilling into the oven and it also makes it easier to take out of the oven.
11. Bake for 35 to 40 minutes until golden and delicious.
12. Make sure you wait at least 20 minutes before you start to devour the crumble.
13. The fruit will be like a volcano and will burn your mouth and is dangerously hot.
14. Serve with ice-cream, cream or custard or even a delicious fresh yoghurt with more berries sprinkled on top for added yumminess!

Yumminess!

Banana Bread

INGREDIENTS

300g Self Raising Flour
100g Caster sugar
50g Soft Brown Sugar
1 tsp Baking powder
1 tsp Bicarbonate of soda
2 Large Eggs
2 Bananas (Not Green, nice and ripe flecks of brown on skin)
2 tsp Vanilla extract
150ml Sunflower oil
100g Chocolate chips (Dark 55%)

METHOD

1. Preheat oven to 180C/350 F/Gas 4.
2. Line a 2lb loaf tin or 12 muffin cases.
3. Whisk together the flour, sugars, baking powder and baking soda.
4. Mash the bananas, vanilla extract, egg, oil and vanilla extract.
5. Add the wet to the dry ingredients and stir until combined.
6. Fold in the chocolate chips but leave a few to scatter on top. Boom!!!
7. Bake in the oven for 35-40 minutes. It can take up to 45 minutes so check after 35 minutes. It will be cooked if a skewer inserted into the pastry comes out clean.
8. Leave to cool for 30 minutes before cutting.

Trish's Top Tip

To ripen bananas preheat oven to 150C and place bananas on a baking tray. Do not remove skins. Bake for 10-15 minutes until the skin turns brown. Ovens vary so it could take longer. If you aren't going to use the ripened bananas, peel and chop them and put in a freezer bag and use for banana bread!

Get some in ma belly!

Battenburg Cake

INGREDIENTS

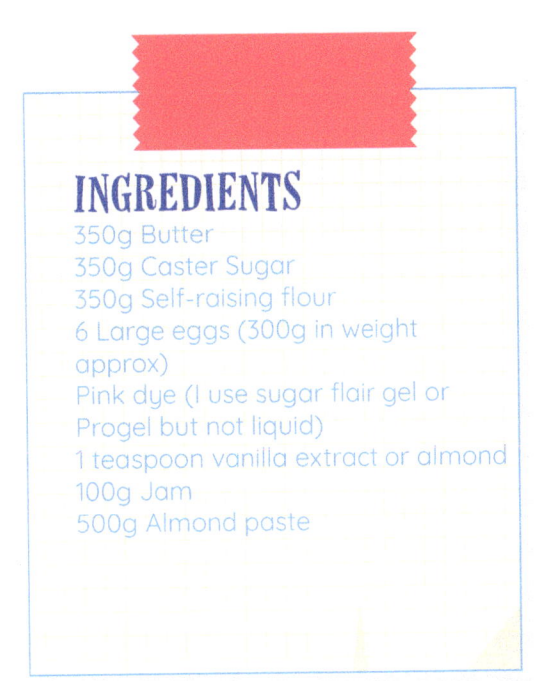

350g Butter
350g Caster Sugar
350g Self-raising flour
6 Large eggs (300g in weight approx)
Pink dye (I use sugar flair gel or Progel but not liquid)
1 teaspoon vanilla extract or almond
100g Jam
500g Almond paste

METHOD

1. Pre-heat the oven to 180C/350F/Gas 4..
2. Line a square 8" tin with parchment paper and make a partition running down the centre as you will be baking two separate loaf cakes.
3. You can create your own partition by double folding foil to fit snugly into the tin so you have a separate compartment for each batter as it bakes. You can slip some cardboard in between the foil to add stability to the cakes when baking.
4. Beat the butter and sugar until blended and then add in gradually all the flour followed by the eggs and extract of almond (if using) Make sure you scrape down if needed to blend well.
5. You should have approximately 1300g of batter so you will need to weigh out 650g for vanilla part and the remaining batter will be dyed pink (or your preferred colour).
6. Try not to use liquid colour as it will affect the batter, gels or pastes work better.
7. Fill each compartment with batter and bake for 45 minutes. Once baked leave to cool completely in the tin.
8. Remove cakes from the tin and level off. Trim all the sides of the cakes so you have no cake skin and just fresh sponge showing in all it's glory.
9. Split each loaf cake in half vertically so you now have four long finger rectangles of cake.
10. Starting with the vanilla sponge brush the top and one side with jam, repeat with the pink sponge with corresponding sides. Now stick the vanilla sponge and pink sponge jam sides together. Brush the top of each finger again with jam and then repeat with the other two fingers of cake.
11. Alternate between colours so you have a pink sponge sitting on top of a vanilla sponge and vice versa. You now have a box cake with diagonal colours matching.
12. Coat all sides with jam ready for the almond paste coating.
13. Roll our the almond paste and using a piece of ribbon as a guide, measure the length and width of the Battenburg cake. You can use this quick guide as a guesstimate to see how much more you have to roll out the almond paste.
14. Sit the Battenburg log on the almond paste and roll up carefully to encase the sponge fingers.
15. Pinch the seams of the almond paste together to secure. I used a little crimper or you can just use your fingers. Sprinkle with caster sugar and leave to dry for about an hour before cutting so the almond paste has time to settle. Enjoy with fourteen cups of tea!

Wholewheat Brown Scones

INGREDIENTS
(MAKES 4 LARGE OR 8 MINI)

100g Wholemeal flour
100g Plain Flour
¼ teaspoon salt
¼ teaspoon Bicarbonate of soda
50g Butter (room temp/soft)
1 tablespoon Brown sugar
100ml Buttermilk

METHOD

1. Pre heat the oven to 180C/350F/Gas 4.
2. Lightly dust the baking sheet.
3. Place the flours, bicarbonate of soda and salt into the mixing bowl and lightly blend with your hand.
4. Add the butter and blend into the flour mix gently squeezing the butter through your finger tips with the flour until it resembles breadcrumbs. The blending technique using your finger tips is similar to dealing a pack of cards or "Show me the money".
5. Now add the sugar and mix with your hand.
6. Make a well in the centre and now pour the buttermilk (not all of it) around the bowl and reserve a little as you may not need all the liquid.
7. Use your hand like a claw and blend the dough, not too rough just enough so the dough binds together.
8. On a lightly floured surface knead lightly the dough and shape into a large square to a 2 finger thickness. Cut into square blocks using a plain cutter not fluted as this can seal the edges and prevents a high rise. Think of fairy wings and delicate butterflies as you knead the dough, you need to have a light touch!! No Miss piggy wallops!
9. Bake in the oven for 20-25 minutes at 180C or for less time if you make smaller scones. Keep an eye on them. You'll know when they're done as if you tap the underside of the scone you should have a hollow sound.

Trish's Top Tip

10. Before you add the buttermilk blend....
11. Add some dried or fresh herbs... Rosemary, thyme or Italian seasoning etc.
12. Add some texture... Chopped nuts, walnuts, sun-dried tomatoes, olives etc.
13. Add spices ¼ teaspoon of cinnamon, or ¼ teaspoon of chill flakes, ¼ teaspoon dried mustard or ¼ teaspoon garlic powder etc.
14. For cheese and chive scones, add chopped chives to your flour mix and then grate 50g cheddar cheese but reduce your butter to 25g. Sprinkle with some grated cheddar to get a cheesy crust... the list is endless.
15. Tiny scones served with smoked salmon and sour cream or cream cheese with sprinkle of chives make for perfect pre-dinner party nibbles.

Party nibbles ready!

Carrot Cake

INGREDIENTS

100g Wholemeal Flour
100g Self-Raising Flour
2 tsp Baking powder
1 tsp ground cinnamon
1 tsp mixed spice
140g Brown sugar
5 Fl oz sunflower oil (¼ pint)
2 large eggs (Lightly beaten)
250g grated carrots
Grated zest of 1 large orange and juice (optional)

METHOD

1. Preheat the oven to 180C/350F/Gas 4.
2. Grease and line the base and sides of a 2lb loaf tin with baking parchment.
3. In a large bowl mix all the dry ingredients, flour, baking powder, sugar and spices.
4. Pour in the oil and add the eggs. Lightly mix and stir in the grated carrots, orange juice and rind.
5. The mixture will be fairly soft and almost runny.
6. Pour the mixture into the prepared tin and bake for 45-50 minutes until it feels firm and springy when you press it in the centre. Cool in the tin for 5 minutes, then turn it out, and cool on a wire rack.
7. Also makes 12 cupcakes.

CREAM CHEESE BUTTERCREAM

1. 225g Cream Cheese
2. 80g Butter (Softened)
3. 550g Icing sugar
4. 1 teaspoon vanilla extract
5. Add the cream cheese and butter to a large mixer and beat until combined.
6. Slowly add the icing sugar, about half to start with and mix well.
7. Add the vanilla extract.
8. Add more or less of the icing sugar depending on your desired consistency.

Courgette & Chocolate Chip Loaf

INGREDIENTS
(SERVES 12)

200g Plain flour
1 teaspoon Bicarbonate of soda
40g Cocoa Powder
120g Dark brown sugar
2 Eggs (Large)
55g Sunflower oil
55g Melted butter
1 teaspoon Vanilla bean paste
(Or two teaspoons vanilla extract)
1 Medium courgette (About 250g/300g grated)
200g Chocolate chips (Milk, dark or White or mixture)
(Reserve about 30g to sprinkle on top)

METHOD

1. Pre-heat the oven to 180C/350F/Gas 4.
2. Blend the flour, bicarbonate of soda and cocoa in a bowl and set aside.
3. In another bowl whisk the eggs, vanilla paste, oil, melted butter and brown sugar.
4. Add the dry ingredients to the wet ingredients and mix until combined.
5. Add the grated courgette and stir in the chocolate chips making sure you reserve a few to sprinkle on top.
6. Pour mixture into a 2lb loaf tin and bake for 50-60 minutes until a toothpick inserted comes out clean and no sticky cake batter is left.
7. Leave cool in the tin for 15 minutes before removing to cool on a rack. Cut into thick slices.
8. Divine serve with a scoop of ice cream or blend mascarpone with a little cream, swirled with some vanilla paste or smear with some Nutella for decadence.

Chocolate & Vanilla Marble Loaf

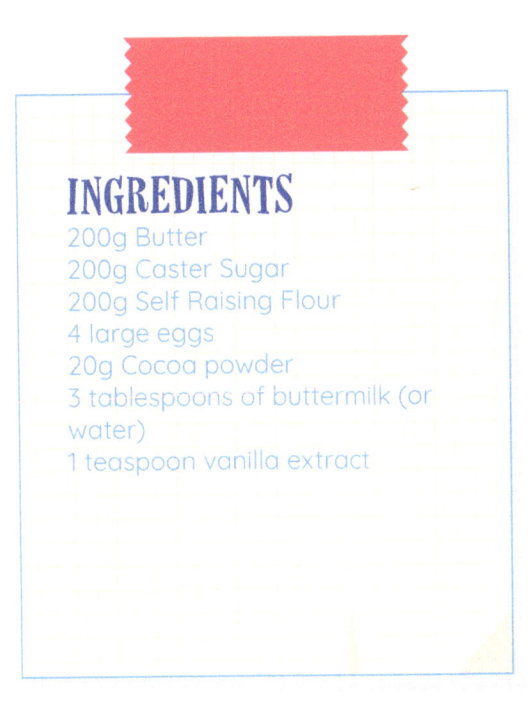

INGREDIENTS
200g Butter
200g Caster Sugar
200g Self Raising Flour
4 large eggs
20g Cocoa powder
3 tablespoons of buttermilk (or water)
1 teaspoon vanilla extract

METHOD

1. Pre heat the oven to 180C/350F/Gas 4.
2. Prepare a 2lb loaf tin with greaseproof paper.
3. Beat the butter and sugar until blended.
4. Next add the flour... say what!!! ... You heard me! ..Add the flour next (makes a huge difference in the sponge and prevents curdling!).
5. Next add the eggs one at a time and then the vanilla extract.
6. Scrape down and mix for about half a minute or until completely mixed through.
7. Divide the mix between two bowls, approximately 400g of batter in each bowl more or less.
8. You should have two bowls of equal batter.
9. Now add the buttermilk to the cocoa powder and mix to a paste. This makes it much easier to blend with the vanilla batter and prevents the cocoa drying out the bake.
10. Add the chocolate paste to one of the measured bowls of vanilla batter and mix until completely incorporated and this now becomes the chocolate sponge.
11. Take a spoon of each batter and dollop it in the tin, overlapping each batter on itself so you have a mixture of vanilla and chocolate, not blending but kissing each other!
12. Bake in a pre-heated oven at 180C for 40-45 minutes until skewer comes out clean, if not put back in the oven for another 5 minutes. Yum diddle dee yum!

Ka-Boom your cake is done!

Breakfast Cinnamon Swirl Sponge

INGREDIENTS
120g Caster sugar
225g Self-raising flour
1 teaspoon baking powder
180ml Buttermilk
1 large eggs
60ml sunflower oil
½ teaspoon almond extract (optional)

CINNAMON SWIRL
60g really soft butter
45g brown sugar
2 teaspoons Plain Flour
1½ teaspoons cinnamon

ICING
60g Icing sugar
1- 1½ tablespoons milk

METHOD

1. Beat the soft butter, brown sugar, flour and cinnamon in a small bowl until lovely and soft, soft enough so you'll be able to pipe directly into the sponge.
2. Transfer the filling to the piping bag and set aside.
3. Pre-heat the oven to 180C and line an 8" round cake tin.
4. In a medium bowl, whisk together the dry ingredients.
5. In a large jug, whisk together milk, eggs, oil and extract (if using).
6. Pour the wet ingredients onto the dry ingredients and stir until you have a smooth batter. Try not to over mix.
7. Pour the batter into the cake tin and this is where the fun begins...
8. Starting in the middle of the cake, like a bullseye, pipe the cinnamon filling (that you prepared earlier) in a spiral pattern.
9. Slightly submerge the piping bag in the cake batter as you pipe, this ensures the cinnamon flavour is injected right into the cake.
10. Round and round you go in a circle as you create that signature cinnamon swirl.
11. Bake at 180C for about 30-35 minutes and the house will fill of cinnamon, sugar and spice and all things nice!
12. Once baked, leave in the cake tin for a few minutes to settle. Run a knife around the tin and invert on a cooling rack.
13. Next prepare a simple glacé icing by whisking icing sugar and milk until a smooth glaze. While the cake is still warm pour over the glaze.
14. Store in an airtight container for up to three days if it lasts that long!

Absolutely divine!

Cranberry & Orange Loaf

INGREDIENTS
250g Plain Flour
1 teaspoon baking powder
200g caster sugar
Zest of 1 orange
180ml Buttermilk
120ml Sunflower oil
2 eggs (Large)
Juice of half an orange (1½- 2 tablespoons)
½ teaspoon vanilla extract
150g Cranberries or raspberries or blueberries
(I used frozen)

ICING
100g of icing sugar
Juice of half an orange (about 1½- 2 tablespoons)
1 teaspoon orange zest

METHOD

1. Pre-heat the oven to 180C.
2. Line a 2lb loaf tin.
3. In a large mixing bowl add the dry ingredients, flour, baking powder, caster sugar, zest of orange and weighed fruit. Stir to combine, making sure you coat all the fruit so it doesn't sink to the bottom.
4. In a jug add the wet ingredients, egg, buttermilk, vanilla extract, orange juice and oil.
5. Pour the wet ingredients onto the dry ingredients and stir.
6. Bake for 45-50 minutes in a lined 2lb loaf tin.

Trish's Top Tip

You can also use fruit like blueberries and raspberries, which are lovely with grated zest of lemon. Change the vanilla extract to almond extract for a different twist.

KA-Boom! You're done #mic drop

Rich Fruit Cake

INGREDIENTS

280g Butter
280g Brown Sugar
60g Chopped tinned strawberries (strained)
100g Melted 55% dark chocolate
375g Plain Flour
2 teaspoons mixed spice
4 Large eggs

FRUIT MIX—STEEP OVERNIGHT

450g Sultanas
450g Raisins
100g Glacé cherries
50g Dried Apricots
50g Cranberries
30g Chopped dates
Zest and Juice of two oranges
80ml Whisky (Brandy or rum

METHOD

1. Pre-heat the oven to 140C and line the 8" round tin with baking parchment.
2. Put the softened butter and sugar into the mixer and beat until smooth.
3. Add the melted chocolate and chopped tinned strawberries (strained).
4. Add the dry mix of flour and spice before you add the eggs as this helps prevent the mix from curdling.
5. Add the eggs one by one until completely combined. Scrape down the bowl if needs be so you have a smooth batter.
6. Add the soaked fruit in thirds so you're not overwhelmed with too much fruit while trying to mix the batter. Alternatively, transfer to a larger bowl to make life easier.
7. Dollop the batter into the tin and indent a hollow in the centre of the batter to allow the cake to rise and keep the top level.
8. Place in a pre-heated oven at 140C and immediately drop the temperature to 130C once the cake goes in.
9. Low and slow gets this cake baked in 4 ½ hours or if you continue to bake at 140C, it will take 3 ½ hours. The choice is yours.
10. The cake is done once it's firm to the touch and a skewer inserted in the centre comes out clean and it also stops singing!!! If you put your ear to the cake you shouldn't hear any giggle gaggle (new word!) of sounds from the fruit cake.
11. I like to bake on a low setting so I have no fear of the cake over baking and drying out.
12. Once out of the oven, leave it 30 minutes before adding a tablespoon of whisky to the top.
13. Leave in the tin overnight. Once completely cold, remove from the tin (keep the original lining) and wrap in greaseproof paper and a layer of foil.
14. Maybe once or twice over the weeks, feed it with a little more whisky. Do not pierce the cake with a skewer just gently pour whisky on the top of the cake and allow it to soak in.
15. Wrap the cake up again tightly and store in a dry cool place.
16. Closer to the time you want to ice it, feed it once more.
17. Don't keep feeding the cake or you'll end up with a plum pudding style fruit cake which can become stodgy.
18. This cake keeps well for weeks if not months once stored correctly. Perfect for any celebration.

Gingerbread Cake

INGREDIENTS

225g Self-raising flour
1 teaspoon Bicarbonate of soda
1 tablespoon Ground ginger
1 teaspoon Mixed spice
1 teaspoon Cinnamon
115g Butter
115g Black Treacle
115g Golden syrup
115g Dark Brown sugar
275ml Milk (any milk will do)
1 large egg

METHOD

1. Pre-heat the oven to 180C/350F/Gas4.
2. Line a 9" square tin.
3. Mix the self-raising flour, bicarbonate of soda, ginger, cinnamon and mixed spice and stir until well blended.
4. Next add the butter to the flour mix and blend with your fingers until fine breadcrumbs.
5. Warm the milk in a jug so it will be able to dissolve the brown sugar. I microwave my milk for 50 seconds (that may vary microwave to microwave) or you can put in a saucepan to warm through.
6. Pour the warm milk over the brown sugar and stir until dissolved.
7. Put the treacle and golden syrup into a microwavable container and heat at 1 minute just enough to soften and warm through.
8. Stirring the flour, pour in the milk and sugar mix and gently whisk, followed by the golden syrup and black treacle and lastly the egg.
9. Make sure all the lumps and bumps are gone and you have a smooth batter. It is very runny so don't panic.
10. Pour the delicious batter into the prepared tin and transfer to the pre-heated oven at 180C for 40-45 minutes.
11. I love using a larger tin rather than a 2lb loaf tin as I get more bang for my buck.
12. The cake cooks in exactly 40 minutes in my oven. It may take a little longer as ovens vary.
13. If you can, leave 24 hours before you devour as the spices develop overnight and even nicer to eat.

Trish's Top Tip

This recipe can be baked in ...two 1lb loaf tins or one large 2lb loaf tin if you have high sides.
The tin must have high sides or it will spill over in the 2lb tin or worse.... sink in the middle with too much batter!!
Perfect as a traybake in a 9" square tin.

Delish!

Jaffa Orange Jelly Cakes

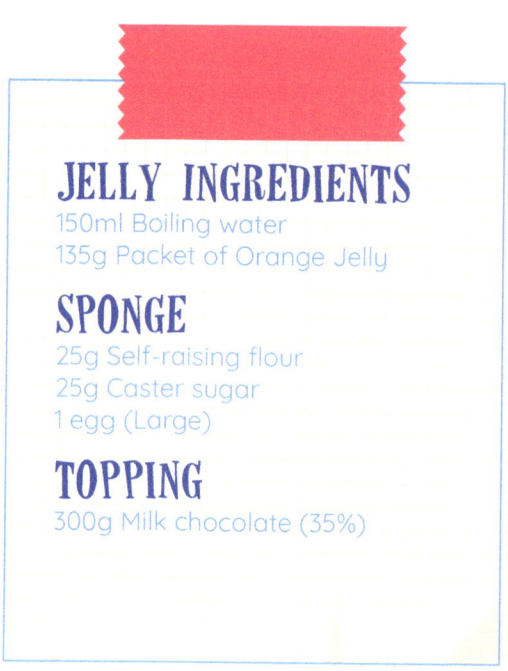

JELLY INGREDIENTS
150ml Boiling water
135g Packet of Orange Jelly

SPONGE
25g Self-raising flour
25g Caster sugar
1 egg (Large)

TOPPING
300g Milk chocolate (35%)

METHOD

1. Pre-heat for oven to 160C/325F/Gas 3.
2. Prepare the jelly the day before to speed things up.
3. Pour 150ml of boiling water into a jug. Cut up the jelly cubes and add to the boiling water. Stir until jelly is dissolved and melted.
4. Using a tablespoon, fill two cupcakes trays with the jelly solution, a tablespoon at a time or pour onto a swiss-roll tray and leave set for a few hours in the fridge.
5. Lightly oil the tray to prevent sticking with either sunflower oil or coconut oil, not butter!
6. Pour egg into the mixer with a whisk attachment along with the caster sugar. Whisk for about 3-4 minutes to get a soft sponge like fluffy batter. You should be able to swirl a figure of eight in the batter using the whisk. If not return to the mixer and whisk again for another minute or two.
7. Once done, sprinkle in the flour on the back of a spoon. This helps prevent the weight of the flour hitting the sponge and deflating the airy sponge mixture.
8. Blend well with the spoon until thoroughly mixed and no flour bits are left behind.
9. Spoon the batter into a prepared cupcake tray (lightly oiled with sunflower oil or coconut oil to prevent sticking.) I use a mini cookie scoop but a tablespoon will do.
10. Bake in a pre-heated oven for 7 minutes and check at 6 minutes as you are looking for a very light golden colour.
11. Once baked, remove from the tin and let cool on a rack.
12. While the sponges are cooling, check on the jelly discs. They should be set by now if you made the jelly the night before or first thing in the morning.
13. Remove a jelly disc and cut to shape, slightly smaller than the sponge and smother with melted chocolate. Using a fork wait a minute or two and indent each Jaffa with a fork to leave an impression and signature Jaffa style marking.

Trish's Top Tip

Any left over jelly discs can be used to coat a traditional digestive biscuit or favourite cookie of choice and covered with chocolate so no discs are left out! I also used a sphere silicone mould with melted jelly to create a domed Jaffa cake instead as seen in the background photo.

Lemon Drizzle Cake

INGREDIENTS
225g Soft Butter
225g Caster Sugar
225g Self-raising flour
4 Large eggs
Zest of two lemons

DRIZZLE GLAZE
75g Caster Sugar
150g Icing Sugar
Juice of two lemons (use the lemons you zested!)

METHOD

1. Pre-heat the oven to 180C/350F/Gas 4.
2. Line the loaf tin (one 2lb loaf tin or two 1lb tins).
3. Beat the sugar and butter together until light and fluffy.
4. While you're waiting for the butter and sugar to mix, zest two lemons into the flour and blend. The smell will be heavenly!
5. Next add the flour to the butter and sugar mix until completely mixed through (adding the flour at this stage prevents the batter from curdling).
6. Scrape down the bowl and gradually add one egg at a time to mix through the batter. Ta-dah you're done!
7. Dollop the batter into the prepared tin or tins.
8. You can either use a 2lb loaf tin or 2 x 1lb loaf tins.
9. I prefer to use the latter as you get two small loafs with one mix and they bake faster.
10. 1lb loaf tins will bake in 35 minutes at 180C and the 2lb loaf tin will bake in 45 minutes to an hour.
11. Once the loaves are baked, immediately poke each loaf with a thin wooden skewer and create some pockets so the lemon drizzle can soak into the warm sponges straight out of the oven.
12. Making the glaze is as easy as 1,2,3...
13. In a little bowl mix the icing sugar, lemon juice and caster sugar and stir!
14. Now pour that delicious glaze slowly over the lemon cake to make sure it seeps into every nook and cranny and leave no poked hole unfilled! The hot sponge will soak up all the delicious sweet goodness from the lemon icing sugar and the caster sugar will leave a lovely sweet crunchy topping when the loaf cools! Or split the glaze between the two loafs to get more bang for your buck!

Trish's Top Tip

Make sure you line the tin as any of that lemon syrup will remain in the cake rather than seeping through the tin and sticking.

Ka-Boom your cake is done!

Lemon Meringue Pie

SHORTCRUST PASTRY INGREDIENTS

180g Plain Flour
100g Cold Butter (Salted)
1 egg yolk
50g Caster sugar
2 or 3 tablespoon cold water (I used two)

FILLING

100g Caster Sugar
2 tablespoons Cornflour
Juice of 2 large lemons (approx 100ml)
200ml Orange juice
 (I used juice of one large orange then made up the rest with carton orange juice)
85g Butter (Diced)
3 egg Yolks + one full egg (whisked together)

MERINGUE

200g Caster Sugar
2 teaspoons cornflour (gives that lovely marshmallow fluffy centre)
4 egg whites

METHOD

1. Pre heat the oven to 180C/350F/Gas 4 and grease the 9" loose bottomed flan tin.
2. Add the butter and blend into the flour mix gently squeezing the butter through your finger tips with the flour until it resembles breadcrumbs. The blending technique using your finger tips is similar to dealing a pack of cards or "Show me the money".
3. Add the sugar.
4. Make a well in the centre of the flour butter mix and add the egg yolk.
5. Sprinkle the cold water around the bowl and use a butter knife to blend in a criss cross pattern across the bowl to represent the mixing blade. I don't use my hand until I can see the pastry come together in clumps, the colour changes too as the butter is mixed and egg yolk to a pale yellow.
6. Now's the time to go in with the hand like a claw and mix the dough. Keep your hand stiff as you move around the bowl and the pastry will come together in a clump. You can start a gentle knead with your hand still in the bowl to bring the dough together.
7. Pastry done ... Ka-Boom!
8. Sprinkle some flour on the worktop and roll out you dough.
9. Now any normal person would let this pastry chill for 30 minutes but then again I'm not normal. Roll out the dough immediately to fit the round 9" flan tin. Using the rolling pin, roll up and down and move the pastry around, so up down and turn it around. So just think from 12 O'Clock to 6 O'Clock and twist the pastry each time so it doesn't stick on the worktop.
10. Use the rolling pin as a guide to roll the pastry back on to the rolling pin so you can lift in place and cover the tin. I use a 9" loose bottomed flan tin. Prick the pastry base with a fork on the base and along the sides.
11. Now you can chill the pastry for 30 minutes to an hour to settle so the pastry doesn't shrink when baked.
12. Bake the pastry case "blind" which means ... place some foil directly onto the flan tin to create a blanket of foil and weigh down with either ceramic beans or dry beans or even rice.
13. Bake for 15 minutes, then take out of the oven and remove the foil (be careful as the foil is hot and the beans are mobile!!!) and bake for another 5-8 minutes until the pastry is pale golden and cooked. When the pastry case is completely cold, fill with the prepared filling.

Lemon Meringue Pie Continued ->

LEMON MERINGUE PIE FILLING

14. Place the cornflour and caster sugar in a saucepan and give it a good blend to get out any lumps and bumps.
15. Slowly add in the lemon juice to blend along with the orange juice and set on a low heat to thicken. This will only take a few minutes on a medium heat.
16. Once the mixture comes to a slow boil and bubble this will activate the cornflour and the mixture will thicken.
17. Immediately take it off the heat and slowly plop the butter into the pot, bit by bit melting into this delicious lemon soup!
18. Whisk the egg yolks and gradually add some of the hot lemon filling into the egg mix first, to prevent a scrambled egg pie! (If you were to put the egg directly into the hot "lemon soup" the egg would immediately start to set and you will have little nibs of cooked egg floating in the meringue filling like scrambled egg... not on my watch!).
19. Now that you have mixed a little hot "lemon filling" into the egg mixture, you can now slowly add all the egg mixture back to the rest of the lemon filling and bring it back to the heat to thicken up.
20. The lemon filling is too runny so the egg now needs to cook off and thicken up.
21. The meringue filling is done once it plip plops (that's a real word!) off the spoon You need to see a "Plip plop" off the spoon or spatula.
22. Turn off the heat and transfer the delicious lemon filling into the prepared pastry case. Leave to cool.
23. You must leave the filling cool for a least an hour before you whip the meringue topping. If you were to add the whipped meringue at this stage when the filling is hot you will deflate the meringue.

MERINGUE TOPPING INGREDIENTS AND METHOD

200g Caster Sugar
2 teaspoons Cornflour
4 Egg whites

24. Make sure the mixer is deliciously clean. Any hint of grease spells disaster for you meringue!
25. Drop a few squeezes of lemon into the bowl and wipe away with some kitchen paper will get rid of any grease.
26. Whisk the egg whites on medium setting until you get a frothy foam. Slowly add the caster sugar until you get soft peaks, little by little until. Once absorbed turn the mixer up a little and now add the cornflour. Another good whisk and the egg whites will turn glossy and shiny, perfect!
27. Cornflour once added will give that spring spong marshmallow texture to the lemon meringue pie.
28. Scoop and dollop out the meringue on top of the prepared pastry shell with the lemon filling and slather the meringue with the palette knife to fill in all the cracks and crannies so no peek-a-boo spots left for oozing lemon filling to escape.
29. Bake in a pre-heated oven for 20-25 minutes until the crisp lemon meringue pie is golden and glows!
30. Leave set and cool for 30 minutes before you dive into the pillowy deliciousness..

Dive into the pillowy deliciousness!

Lemon Poppy Seed Cake

INGREDIENTS
200g Caster Sugar
100g Plain Flour
100g Wholemeal flour
100ml of Natural Yoghurt
1 tablespoon of poppy seeds
2 teaspoons baking powder
3 eggs (Large)
100ml Sunflower Oil
1 teaspoon vanilla extract
Lemon Zest from two lemons

ICING
100g Icing Sugar
Juice of ½ lemon or more..
(depends on how thick or runny you like the icing)

METHOD
1. Pre heat the oven to 180C/350F/Gas 4.
2. Line a 2lb loaf tin.
3. In a separate jug add the wet ingredients and whisk together.
4. In a separate bowl add all the dry ingredients together, the flours, sugar, baking powder and poppy seeds and stir to combine.
5. Make a well in the centre of the dry ingredients and add the wet ingredients. Just like a muffin mixture, don't overmix or the cake will get too dense.
6. Pour batter into a 2lb loaf tin and place in the preheated oven and bake for 50 minutes.
7. Once a toothpick comes out clean, rest the loaf on a rack and wait until it's cool to pour the glacé icing …. Droooool…..

ICING

Blend the icing sugar with half the lemon juice in a little bowl and stir until completely mixed. If a little stiff, add more lemon juice to the required constituency. Pour or spread on top of the freshly baked loaf.

#Droooool

Lemon Swissroll

INGREDIENTS
4 Large Eggs
110g Caster Sugar
75g Plain Flour
9" x 13" Swissroll tin

METHOD

1. Pre heat the oven to 180C/350F/Gas 4.
2. Grease and line the tray with parchment.
3. Warm up the caster sugar by placing the sugar on some parchment paper on a baking tray and heating in the oven for 4 minutes.... Set the timer!!!
4. In the meantime whip the whole eggs in the mixer for about 2 minutes and then add all the warmed sugar. Make sure you're careful when taking the warm sugar out of the oven, use oven gloves! The warmed sugar helps volumise the eggs and create a mountain of air and deliciousness.. ness ! Lol
5. This needs to beat for about 4 minutes on high until you get the figure of eight ... meaning ... when you lift the whisk you should be able to create an imaginary figure of eight with the whisk using wrist action.
6. Next get a metal spoon and sprinkle the sieved flour on to the back of the spoon before you add to the batter mix so it prevents the batter mix from collapsing from the weight of the flour.
7. Stir slowly so all the flour is incorporated and there are no visible lumps.
8. Pour the delicious light and fluffy angel delight of a batter into the tray and using a knife spread out the batter while tilting the tray to help it fall into place and make sure it's evenly spread.
9. Bake in the pre heated oven for 10-12minutes until light and golden.
10. Prepare a sheet of greaseproof paper sprinkled with caster sugar.
11. Once the swissroll is out of the oven, invert the tray directly on top of the greaseproof while warm. Peel the baking paper off the sponge and roll up the greaseproof paper and leave the swissroll cool. I wrap mine in a clean tea towel like a blanket so to trap the heat and keep the moisture in so you have a lovely spring sprong sponge!
12. Once cool, unroll the greaseproof and spread the jam and cream and roll up into a magnificent swissroll. Sprinkle with icing sugar and decorate if you wish with a dollop of cream or swirls of piped cream and fruit for decoration.
13. Chill in the fridge to firm before serving and enjoy!

FILLING
250ml of whipped cream
Lemon curd of jam of your choice

Enjoy!

Passion Fruit & Lemon Meringue Roulade

INGREDIENTS
280g Caster sugar
5 egg whites
½ teaspoon cream of tartar or lemon juice
6g Vera Miklas Dried Passion fruit (Optional) OR
20g Vera Miklas Dried Raspberry powder (Optional)
(Blitz dried raspberries in food processor for a powder)

FILLING
250ml whipped cream
Lemon curd

ICING
225g Caster sugar
2 tablespoons cornflour
100ml fresh lemon juice or limes
200ml orange juice
100g Butter
5 egg yolks

METHOD
1. Pre heat the oven to 180C/350F/Gas 4.
2. Line a 9x 13 inch Swiss-roll tin with non stick parchment paper.
3. Make sure the mixer is deliciously clean. Any hint of grease spells disaster for the meringue!
4. Drop a few squeezes of lemon into the bowl and wipe with some kitchen paper to get rid of any grease.
5. Whisk the egg whites on medium until you get a frothy foam. Next add the cream of tartar until you get soft peaks. Once absorbed turn the mixer up a little and now add the caster sugar, little by little and whisk until the egg whites turn glossy and stiff peaks have formed.
6. You should be able to turn the bowl upside down and hold over your head.... when stiff peaks have developed. If not you've got a fab meringue hairdo!! Lol
7. At this stage you can blend in the dried passion fruit sprinkles or dried raspberries into the meringue mix for some added "zing" to the roulade.
8. Scoop and dollop out the meringue on to the tray. Slather the meringue with the palette knife to fill in all the cracks and crannies on the tray.
9. Bake in a pre-heated oven for 20 minutes until the crisp meringue pie is golden and puffed up.
10. Leave set and cool for 10 minutes before you fill with lemon curd and cream or filling of your choice. Add some passion fruit coulis for extra bite. Coulis is found in most supermarkets.

LEMON CURD FILLING
1. Place the cornflour and caster sugar in a saucepan and give it a good blend to get out any lumps and bumps.
2. Slowly add in the lemon juice to blend along with the orange juice and set on a low heat to thicken. This will only take a few minutes on a medium heat.
3. Once the mixture comes to a slow boil and bubble this will activate the cornflour and the mixture will thicken.
4. Immediately take it off the heat and slowly plop the butter into the pot bit by bit melting into this delicious lemon soup!
5. Whisk the egg yolks and gradually add some of the hot lemon filling into the egg mix first to prevent scrambled egg. (If you were to put the egg directly into the hot "lemon soup" the egg would immediately start to set and you will have little nibs of cooked egg floating in the meringue filling like scrambled egg... not on my watch!)
6. Now that you have mixed a little hot "lemon filling" into the egg mixture you can now slowly add all the egg mixture back to the rest of the lemon filling and bring it back to the heat to thicken up. The lemon filling is too runny so the egg now needs to cook off and thicken up.
7. The meringue filling is done once it plip plops (that s a real word!) off the spoon You need to see a "Plip plop" off the spoon or spatula .
8. Turn off the heat and leave to cool before you can use to fill the roulade.
9. You will not use all the lemon curd so pot up in a jam jar or Kilner jar and keep in the fridge for smearing on toast or fresh scones, waffles... the list is endless.

Traditional Irish Scones

INGREDIENTS
500g Self-raising flour
2 tsp baking powder
100g Butter
2 tablespoons caster sugar
1 Egg (Large)
250ml/300ml milk (Depending on size of egg)

METHOD

1. Pre heat the oven to 180C/350F/Gas 4.
2. Add the flour, baking powder and butter into a bowl and blend together with your finger tips, gently squeezing the butter through your finger tips with the flour until it resembles breadcrumbs. The blending technique using your finger tips is similar to dealing a pack of cards or "Show me the money".
3. Now add the sugar and mix with your hand.
4. Make a well in the centre and crack in an egg. Now pour the milk (not all of it) around the bowl and reserve about 50mls as you may not need all the liquid depending on the size of the egg.
5. Make a claw shape with your hand and blend the dough but not too rough just enough so the dough binds together.
6. On a lightly floured surface knead lightly the dough to a 2" thickness and cut into rounds with a plain cutter not fluted as this can seal the edges and prevents a high rise. Think of fairy wings and delicate butterflies as you knead the dough. You need to have a light touch!! Not Miss piggy wallops!
7. Place on a baking tray sprinkled with flour and bake for 20-25 minutes.

Trish's Top Tip

** To make Gluten free just use gluten free flour and baking powder along with two teaspoons of Xanthum gum.

Yummy, yummy, yummy

Tea Brack

INGREDIENTS

300g Mixed fruit (Sultanas and Raisins)
200g Brown Sugar
225g Self-Raising Flour
300ml tea....(BARRYS TEA in my house!)
1 Large egg
GLAZE
1 tbsp apricot jam
1 tsp water

METHOD

1. Heat oven to 180C/350F/Gas 4.
2. Measure out 300ml of boiling water into a jug. Pop a tea bag into a jug containing 300mls of boiling water. Stir and leave to stew for about 10 minutes. Make yourself a brew while you're at it!
3. Pour the cooled tea including the teabag over the fruit and leave to soak over night.
4. The next day preheat the oven to 180C/350F or gas mark 4.
5. With the mixed fruit soaked overnight ... remove the tea bag from the mixed fruit which has soaked overnight and stir in the weighed out brown sugar into the same bowl (saves washing up!).
6. Fold half the flour into the bowl and mix well before adding all the egg and then the remaining flour. Mix well.
7. Pour into a 2lb loaf tin lined with greaseproof paper. KA-BOOM you're done!
8. Bake for about 45 minutes to an hour depends on how wet the mix is and the size of the egg. It could take up to an hour before the skewer comes out clean.
9. Check the brack after an hour by sticking a skewer into the middle of the cake. If it comes out clean the brack is done. If the batter is a little sticky put it back in the oven for another 5 minutes and check again.
10. Heat the apricot jam in the microwave with a teaspoon of water for 30 seconds or 1 minute until melted and glaze the brack.

Trish's Top Tip

If you want to go posh, you can use Earl Grey tea to give a perfumed flavour to the brack and use a saucer while drinking !

#pinkiesout

Victoria Meringue Sponge

VICTORIA SPONGE
100g Caster Sugar
100g Soft Butter
100g Self-raising flour
2 Large eggs
1 teaspoon Baking powder

MERINGUE LAYER
200g Caster sugar
1 teaspoon cream of tartar
4 Large egg whites

FILLING
250g Cream
200g or more of fresh or frozen fruit of choice

METHOD

1. Preheat the oven to 160C/320F/Gas 3.
2. Line an 8 inch or 2 sandwich tins with baking parchment.
3. Make the meringue mix first as you'll use the bowl again for the Victoria batter.
4. Use a few drops of lemon juice to remove any grease from the bowl before you whisk the egg whites. Just wipe the inside with some lemon juice with a paper towel or kitchen paper. It's important to make sure no grease is present or the egg whites won't whip.
5. In a standalone mixer or hand mixer whisk the egg whites until frothy, you'll see a foam starting and gradually the foam increases in volume. Sprinkle in the cream of tartar to stabilise the egg white mix so it doesn't deflate and collapse.
6. Whisk for a few seconds more at a high speed and slowly add the caster sugar spoon by spoon until you get lovely glossy meringue mix.
7. You should be able to put the bowl of meringue over your head without any fear of it sliding and landing on your head!
8. Scape out the meringue into a separate bowl, using the same bowl you mixed the meringue in. Now add all the ingredients for the Victoria sponge… saves washing up! Beat the sponge mix for less than a minute just to combine. It's important that the butter is so soft you could press your finger through. This is an all in one method, but not suitable for a traditional sponge. There is a recipe for a Victoria sponge on the next page as it uses a different technique!

Meringue Sponge Continued ->

ASSEMBLY

9. Weigh out the batter for each tin so you now have two tins of cake batter evenly spread. Split the meringue mix between the two tins and dollop the mixture directly on top of the sponge batter and again spread out evenly.
10. Bake in a preheated oven at 160C for 25 minutes and no more. Leave to sit for a few minutes after baking before running a knife around the rim of the cake tin to release.
11. Be gentle as the meringue mix will inflate and then deflate as it's still fragile.
12. I use a cooling rack covered with a double layer of parchment to prevent any score lines from the cooling rack compressed on the top of the meringue crust. When you invert the tin, peel back the paper from the cooked sponge. Flip back using another rack like a sandwich for a safe transfer and let it cool.
13. Once cool, put sponge base with the meringue top on a decorative plate. Layer with whipped cream and fresh or frozen fruit. Carefully place next sponge on top so you have the sponge base resting on the fruit and cream and again the meringue on top for decoration. Dollop some cream on top and scatter with more fruit along with a dusting of icing sugar and Ka-Boom! Masterpiece!

Ka-Boom! Masterpiece!

TRAYBAKES & PARTY TREATS

"KNOCK, KNOCK...
WHO'S THERE?
BACON....
BACON WHO?
...BACON A CAKE FOR YOUR BIRTHDAY!"

American Angel Cake

INGREDIENTS
100g Self-raising Flour
2 tablespoons cornflour
120g Icing Sugar
8 Egg whites
1 teaspoon Lemon juice
120g Caster Sugar
1 ½ teaspoons Almond Extract

TOPPING
250ml Cream (Whipped)
250ml Cream
250ml Mascarpone
120g Icing sugar
1 teaspoon of vanilla paste
200g Strawberries
100g Blueberries

METHOD

1. Pre-heat the oven to 180C/350F/Gas 4.
2. Blend the flour, cornflour and icing sugar in a small bowl and stir until combined.
3. DO NOT GREASE THE TIN!
4. Whisk the egg whites until foamy and then add the lemon juice. This helps add volume and stabilises the egg whites. Next add the almond extract.
5. Once you have added the lemon juice slowly, add the caster sugar, one spoonful at a time until it is completely incorporated. Leave whisk for about 5 minutes until the mixture has a glossy shiny appearance and you can hold the bowl over your head without fear of it landing on your head like a shaving foam poo!
6. Next add the flour in three stages. Sprinkle the flour over the back of the spatula to prevent the egg whites from collapsing.
7. Stir the flour in gently each time, until it is completely blended and no flour pockets are visible.
8. Pour the batter into the tin, paddle right to the edges using the spatula and even out until level.
9. Bake in the preheated oven for 25-30 minutes until golden.
10. Immediately once baked invert the cake tin directly on four cans to prevent the cake from collapsing and leave cool upside down for about 30 minutes to an hour.

TOPPING

11. Slowly whisk the mascarpone until smooth and creamy. Add the icing sugar and slowly add all the cream and whip until soft peaks form.
12. Using a palette knife smooth the icing on top of the cooled Angel cake. Decorate as a US Flag using the blueberries and sliced strawberries.
13. Fill a piping bag with the whipped cream and using a 1M Wilton nozzle, pipe a decorative border around the cake and between the fruit borders to finish the design.

Trish's Top Tip

Do not line or grease the tin. This cake is to be served straight from the tin, decorated and all! It must be inverted upside down to cool so gravity can pull the sponge and prevent collapsing. The cake will fall out if greased.

Ka-Boom... 4th of July Celebrations here I come!

No-Bake Baileys & White Chocolate Cheesecake*

BISCUIT BASE (STEP 1)
225g Chocolate Plain Digestive Biscuits or Gluten Free*
100g Butter
30g Caster Sugar

FILLING
250g Cream cheese
300ml Cream
100g Caster sugar
250g Mascarpone Cheese
200g Belgian white chocolate (melted)
150ml Baileys
1 Sachet gelatine dissolved **see notes

GELATINE MIX*
Weigh our 70ml of cold water in a bowl
Sprinkle the gelatine sachet over the cold water
Leave to bloom for ten minutes until it soaks up all the water

METHOD

STEP 1: BISCUIT BASE

1. Prepare a 9" round loose bottom tin.
2. Grease the base with butter and line the sides only with parchment paper or acetate. This makes life so much easier when removing the cheesecake, trust me!
3. Melt the butter and let cool as you crush the digestive biscuits.
4. Crush the biscuits either by putting into a freezer bag and using a rolling pin to crush or by blitzing in a food processor. Pulse into fine breadcrumbs. I use the latter method as it's faster.
5. Pour the melted butter over the biscuit and blend well.
6. Press the biscuit crumb firmly into the tin and chill to set for at least 15 minutes in the fridge.

STEP 2: FILLING

7. In the mixer add the cream cheese and caster sugar. Beat on a medium speed for 1 minutes until smooth and creamy. Next add the Baileys and scrape down the sides of the bowl if necessary.
8. Add the cream slowly into the mix and beat to a soft whip, this takes about 2 minutes.
9. Melt the chocolate and leave to cool.
10. Stop the mixer, scrape down the sides and now add the mascarpone and blend until smooth.
11. **Microwave gelatine mix for 30 seconds in the microwave making sure it's completely dissolved until the liquid looks clear. Add to the cheesecake mix. The warm gelatine will loosen the cream cheese filling and helps mix the chocolate through.
12. Pour in the melted chocolate and fold by hand.
13. Once mixed pour the cheesecake filling onto the prepared tin and chill overnight.
14. Once chilled, decorate with a dusting of cocoa powder and some white chocolate shavings
15. To ensure a smooth cheesecake, make sure all ingredients are at room temperature before starting.

STEP 3: DECORATION

Cocoa (dusting) 100g white Chocolate shavings
*CAN BE MADE GLUTEN FREE

Ka-Boom your cake is done!

88

Belgian Chocolate Biscuit Cake*

INGREDIENTS

100g Butter
250g Dark chocolate 55%
100g Milk chocolate
150g Digestive Biscuits or GF
100g Mini Marshmallows or GF
100g** Mixed chocolate chips, white, milk and dark (or use a variety, see TIP)
75g Malteesers or GF sweets
3 tablespoons Golden syrup

METHOD

1. I use an 8" Brownie tray lined with greaseproof.
2. Put butter, chocolate and golden syrup together in a microwaveable bowl. Zap in the microwave for one minute.
3. After 1 minute the mixture starts to melt. Give it a good stir and put back in the microwave for another minute. You can an also put the bowl over a pot of simmering water until just about melted. (The residual heat will continue to melt the chocolate so don't overheat).
4. Leave the mix for about a minute or two so the chocolate is warm to the touch but not hot.
5. While you're waiting for the chocolate to cool, break up the digestive biscuits into small bite size pieces. Add the Malteesers and half the marshmallows to the chocolate butter mix.
6. Now give it a good old stir and mix those delicious ingredients together!!
7. Sprinkle with the remainder of the marshmallows and… KA-BOOM your done!
8. Place in the fridge and allow to set which could take about 30 minutes to an hour.

*Trish's Top Tip

You can mix and match a variety of fillings just keep the weight the same! Cranberries, chopped apricots, nuts etc. Go wild and create your own!

CAN BE MADE GLUTEN FREE - Substitute biscuits and sweets to gluten free variety.

Berry Crumble Oat Bars*

SPONGE TOPPING
270g Plain Flour or Gluten Free
1 teaspoon Bicarbonate of soda
250g Caster Sugar
½ teaspoon mixed spice
1 large egg
250ml Natural Yoghurt
140g Butter
Zest of one large orange

CRUMB
115g Butter
150g Plain Flour or Gluten Free
2 tablespoons sugar
50g Oats or Gluten free oats
200g Red Berries (Berries of choice)

METHOD

1. Pre heat the oven to 180C/350F/Gas4
2. Grease a 13x9" tray at least 1.5" or 2" deep
3. Line the tray with parchment.

METHOD (CRUMB)

4. Start with the crumble mix as you don't want the sponge made first hanging around waiting for the crumb topping.
5. To make the crumble, tip the flour into a bowl and blend the butter with your fingertips until it resembles breadcrumbs with a few lumps and bumps of butter still visible. Add the sugar now add the oats.
6. Boom crumb mixture done!! Easy Peasy, now next on to the sponge base....

METHOD (SPONGE)

7. First blend the flour, mixed spice, baking soda and grated zest of the orange in a bowl ready for the mixer.
8. In a stand alone mixer or hand mixer beat the butter and sugar together.
9. Add the egg and blend until completely mixed through, scrap down the bowl.
10. Now add the flour mix, spoon by spoon. Don't forget to scrape down the bowl again if needed and mix until blended.
11. Add the yoghurt and mix thoroughly... Ta-Dah... sponge done!
12. Spread the batter mix over the base of the tin and completely cover from edge to edge with the batter, smoothing out with the back of a spoon or palette knife.
13. Now scatter the berries to cover the sponge and top with the crumble, again completely covering the berries like a blanket of crumb.
14. Bake in a preheated oven for 35/40 minutes. It may even take longer, checking after 30 minutes.
15. It will be done when the sponge springs back from the centre and the edges of the traybake have a lovely golden colour.
16. Leave completely for about 2 hours before you even attempt to cut it as the bars are very fragile once baked but they will set once cooled.

*CAN BE MADE GLUTEN FREE

Try & eat only one... I dare ya!

Berry & Banana Oat Pancakes*

INGREDIENTS
150ml Milk
2 large Eggs
1 Egg White
1 Banana
2 tablespoons 100% Real Maple Syrup
150g Porridge Oats or Gluten Free
2 teaspoons Baking Powder or GF
1 teaspoon Vanilla extract

METHOD

1. In a blender, pour in milk, eggs, egg white, banana, maple syrup, vanilla (optional), rolled oats, baking powder and salt.
2. Blend until smooth.... BOOM...Pancake batter is done!
3. Heat pan over medium heat.
4. Once warmed, spray with non-stick cooking spray or place coconut oil or butter in the pan.
5. Pour pancake batter into the pan in small round circles. You can add some blueberries or whatever fruit tickles your fancy.
6. Cook for 1-2 minutes on one side. Turn over and cook for another 1-2 minutes.
7. Drizzle with real maple syrup and toppings of choice, woohoo! Bon Appetit.

YUMMY TOPPINGS IDEAS:

8. Fresh Berries
9. Chopped nuts and maple syrup (The real stuff! No **mockey-ahhh)
10. Dark Chocolate Chips (55%)
11. Banana Slices

*CAN BE MADE GLUTEN FREE (GF)

Berry Tiramisu

INGREDIENTS

4 tablespoons Liqueur (I use Creme de cassis)
1 packet (20 fingers) of sponge fingers
250g Mascarpone cheese
250ml Cream
200ml Custard (Pre-made to speed thing up!)
2-3 tablespoons Cocoa Powder for decoration
200ml Water
70g Caster Sugar
500g Frozen mixed fruit berries

METHOD

1. Dissolve 200ml of water with 70g of caster sugar and slowly bring to the boil to create a sugar syrup. Let it boil rapidly for about a minute. Turn off the heat and throw in the frozen berries and let them seep until the fruit mixture has gone cold.
2. Once cold, sieve to remove the frozen fruit and you are left with a gorgeous pink bath. Add 2 tablespoons of the cassis and you have a truly berry scrumptious bath for the sponge fingers! The remaining two tablespoons of cassis is added to the custard cream mixture using the same method as outlined for the coffee tiramisu.
3. Layering up is the same. Dip the fingers, smother with the custard cream filling, scatter with fruit and repeat!
4. Same goes for a Pinacolada or Tropical fruit tiramisu, just use pineapple and mango frozen mix, use clear rum for a punch or Malibu or whatever takes your fancy!
5. You hardly taste the alcohol, but it is enough especially if kids are going to enjoy too. By all means kick up the volume regarding the punch of alcohol but not too much as you don't want an overpowering alcohol aftertaste... or maybe you do! Of course you can omit completely too!

Whatever takes your fancy!

Black Forest Cherry Pavlova

INGREDIENTS
4 Egg whites
250g Icing sugar
2 teaspoons Cornflour
3 tablespoons cocoa powder
1 teaspoon Vanilla extract
1 teaspoon White wine vinegar
¼ teaspoon Cream of tartar (or lemon juice will do)
Few drops of lemon juice (to clean the mixer and whisk)

FILLING
500ml whipped cream
1 tablespoon icing sugar
2 tablespoon kirsch or cherry liqueur (optional)
Can of black cherries
100g chocolate shavings
200g Fresh cherries

METHOD

1. Pre-heat the oven to 150C/300F/Gas2.
2. Line two trays with baking non stick parchment paper. Mark out an 8" circle on both trays to use as a guide to fill the meringue.
3. Use a tiny squeeze of lemon juice to clean the whisk and the bowl of the mixer before you start as any traces of grease will kill the meringue!
4. Pour the egg whites into a bowl or mixer and whisk until foamy, next add the cream of tartar or lemon juice (this helps stabilise the eggs and gives volume).
5. Continue to whisk and slowly add the icing sugar, spoon by spoon until completely combined.
6. Gently pour in the vanilla extract, the cornflour and finally the white wine vinegar and whisk until shiny and glossy.
7. You should by now be able to stop the machine and turn the bowl upside down and hold over your head as the meringue is now a thick mousse.
8. Gently sieve the cocoa powder over the meringue and gently stir through, you can either completely blend through or leave pockets of white meringue and cocoa powder swirled through the mix.
9. Using your eye as a guide split the mix into two and divide between the two trays.
10. Dollop the meringue to the edge of the diameter marked on the parchment. Paddle the meringue right to the edges forming a ridge and a slight dip in the middle of the meringue.
11. This will help create a hollow for the whipped cream filling.
12. Place in the pre-heated oven for 45 minutes. Once cooked, leave on the tray to cool completely before transferring to a decorative plate. I use a cake lifter to carefully transfer the delicate meringue so I have no fear of cracking when moving.

FILLING & ASSEMBLY

13. Whip the cream to soft peaks. Drain the cherries and add 2 tablespoons of liqueur, leave sit.
14. Reserve the cherry juice and reduce over a medium heat for about 5-10 minutes until you are left with a sticky thick sauce. Leave to cool.
15. Add a tablespoon of liqueur to the syrup for extra punch!
16. Now to assemble the meringue discs, place a layer of the meringue on the cake stand and smother with whipped cream. Scatter some of the soaked cherries along with a drizzle of the cherry sauce. Sprinkle with chocolate shavings and repeat with the next layer and top with the remaining cream.
17. Dive in head first and eat your way through the Blackforest ...

Cake Pops

INGREDIENTS
300g Cake crumb/trimmings

GANACHE
200g Milk Belgian chocolate
90-100ml cream
Melt 300g Chocolate (for dipping)
Sprinkles

METHOD

1. Make the ganache first by bringing the cream to just boiling point and wait a minute before pouring over the chocolate chips.
2. Wait for a few seconds before stirring completely until you have a smooth satin chocolate soup!
3. Leave to rest for a few minutes until cool.
4. Crumb the cake trimmings into breadcrumbs gently with your finger tips and slowly add about two tablespoons of ganache.
5. Use a fork rather than your hand to start mixing in the ganache so the cake crumb is completely covered and resembles a sticky putty.
6. Using your hands take mini golf ball sizes and mould into shape using a gentle squeeze.
7. If the cake mixture is a little crumbly add a little more ganache.
8. Buttercream is not a great binding agent for cake pops as it begins to soften once taken out of the fridge so the cake pops can lose their stability and crack or break easily.
9. Ganache on the other hand sets hard and stabilises the cake pops once chilled so they can be dipped without fear of falling off their stick.
10. Once you have moulded the cake pops place them on a tray covered with either a silicone mat or a food freezer bag as this make life so much easier when removing them from the fridge. They just "pop" off!
11. Cake pops need to be chilled for at least 30 minutes before attempting to dip as the ganache needs to set.
12. Once chilled dip the cake pop stick or a paper straw into the melted chocolate and insert directly into the middle of the cake pop to anchor the straw into place before you start dipping. Leave for a few seconds for the chocolate to set on the chilled cake pop, it won't take long.
13. Once secured you can now completely dip the cake pop into the chocolate. I like to use a small container as it raises the level of the chocolate and makes it easier to dip. Tilt the container at an angle so it makes life easier to swirl and cover the cake pop with chocolate.
14. Sprinkle with the magical sprinkles and the cake pop is born!
15. To help keep the cake pops all together, I use bamboo sticks stuck into a block of polystyrene. You can easily slide the straw down through the bamboo stick and this helps the straw from bending from the weight of the cake pop and stabilises the cake pop while it drys.
16. I buy eco friendly straws instead of plastic cake pops as they are cheaper and you can also do your bit for the environment. Win-win!

Caramel Squares

MAGIC BASE
225g Plain Flour
175g Butter (very cold butter)
75g Caster sugar

MAGIC FILLING
150g Butter
1 can condensed Milk
100g Golden syrup

MAGIC TOPPING
350g Dark Chocolate 55% or blend (I used 250g milk chocolate and 100g of 70%)
Ok let's start with base.... Its all about the base bout the base no trouble!!
Grease and line the tin, I use a 9 x 13" swissroll tin

METHOD

1. Pre-heat oven to 180C/350F/Gas 4.
2. Now for some easy peasy shortcrust base. Put the cold butter and flour into the food processor and PULSE for a few seconds until the butter has blended like coarse sand. You don't want to overmix. YOU WANT SAND!!
3. Now add the caster sugar for the last pulse. Ka-Boom the sweet shortbread sand mix is now ready. Tip the whole mix on the prepared tray and scatter and spread with your fingers first and then pat with a spoon like you would if making a sand castle.
4. Bake in a preheated oven for 15-20 minutes until golden brown. Check after 15 minutes so it doesn't burn.
5. Make sure you cool the shortbread for at least 15minutes before you start on the caramel filling.

FILLING:

6. Place the condensed milk, butter and golden syrup in a saucepan and gently heat until all the butter has melted.
7. Now turn up the heat and let it begin to bubble and keep that constant bubble for 7 minutes (set the timer!!).
8. Once the time is up, you can check the caramel by testing a teaspoon of it in a glass of ice cold water.
9. The caramel should solidify to a soft paste when merged in the cold water and leave a tacky train on a spoon. Be very careful when pouring the caramel as it is dangerously hot!!
10. Pour onto the shortbread and spread using a palette knife.

TOPPING

11. About 20 minutes after cooling the caramel shortbread, I like to mark out the portions, so when you melt and cover with chocolate, the chocolate guides itself to the markings you have previously made in the caramel. It wiggles itself into the cracks and makes it easier to cut without cracking the chocolate.
12. Melt 350g of chocolate and pour directly on to the cooled caramel shortbread and leave to set.
13. If you're feeling fancy, when you melt the chocolate, lay a chocolate transfer sheet directly on to the melted chocolate and leave to set. The chocolate pattern will show once you've peeled off the transfer and everyone will Oooooooo.... and Ahhhhh... at your masterpiece!

Delish!

Chocolate Brownies*

INGREDIENTS
(SERVES 9)

115g Self raising Flour or Gluten Free flour
25g Cocoa
115g Butter
75g Dark chocolate 55%
2 Large eggs
190g Brown sugar
75g Milk chips for blending
25g Milk chips (optional) for sprinkling

METHOD

1. Preheat oven to 180 C/350F/Gas4.
2. Line a 8 inch square brownie tin.
3. Add the flour, cocoa and sugar in a bowl.
4. In another microwaveable bowl, melt the butter and chocolate by zapping in the microwave for about 40 seconds to a minute depending on the microwave wattage. (Mine is 1100W).
5. Now add the melted butter chocolate mixture (wet ingredients) to the sugar and flour (dry ingredients), mix and stir.
6. Blend in beaten egg and add the 75g chocolate chips and mix.
7. Sprinkle with the remaining 25g of chocolate chips for the top (Optional... who doesn't love optional right!).
8. Spoon the mixture into a tin and bake for 25-30 minutes or until the top forms a crust and the centre is slightly springy and doesn't wobble when shaken!!
9. Cut into 9 squares or smaller for more brownies!
10. Serve warm with ice-cream.

*CAN BE MADE GLUTEN FREE by adding ½ teaspoon Xanthan gum and GF flour

#Masterpiece!

Chocolate Birthday Cake*

INGREDIENTS

250g Plain Flour
80g Cocoa Powder
2 ½ teaspoons baking powder
1 teaspoon bicarbonate of soda
325g Brown Sugar
250ml Buttermilk
185ml Sunflower oil
125ml Strong coffee or
(4 teaspoons instant coffee dissolved in water not boiling, can even be warm)
2 teaspoons vanilla extract
2 large eggs

METHOD

1. Heat oven to 180C /350F/Gas 4.
2. Line the base of 2 x 8" tins or 3 x 6" tins.
3. Combine flour, cocoa powder, baking powder, bicarbonate of soda and sugar in a large bowl.
4. Whisk oil, buttermilk, coffee, vanilla and eggs together in a jug, then pour the wet ingredients into the dry mix and blend well, getting all the lumps and bumps out. Boom! Batter done.
5. Pour the mixture into the tins and bake for 30-35 minutes until a skewer inserted into the centre comes out clean.
6. Leave to cool in the tin until completely cold. This is a lovely soft sponge so handle with care.

BUTTERCREAM FILLING

7. Beat the living daylights out of 250g butter, 500g icing sugar and 50g cocoa along with 2-3 tablespoons of milk. Whip for at least ten minutes for silky smooth buttercream. It's much easier to fill and pipe using a buttercream that is light and airy. Firm buttercream will tear the cake crumb and your sanity!
8. *CAN BE MADE GLUTEN FREE - Substitute Flour and baking powder to GF and add ½ teaspoon Xanthan Gum

Get in ma belly!

Chocolate Mousse*

INGREDIENTS
200g Dark chocolate (55%)
125ml Cream (Softly Whipped)
3 Egg whites (90g)
50g Caster Sugar

METHOD

1. Prepare the cream by softly whipping and leave rest in a bowl.
2. Place the eggs in the mixer and froth until foamy, next add the caster sugar and whisk until soft peaks have formed. It takes about a minute with the mixer on high or full speed.
3. Melt the chocolate in a bowl over some simmering water. Melt until just few nibs of chocolate left and take off the heat. The residual heat will continue to melt the chocolate.
4. You can also melt the chocolate in a microwave. Place the chocolate in a microwaveable container and zap for a minute, then stir and zap for 20 second intervals until completely melted.
5. Pour the melted chocolate into a large bowl as you'll need to incorporate the egg whites along with the cream so it is best suited to a large bowl for mixing.
6. Add a third of the egg whites to the chocolate and blend, followed by another third and blend and finally making sure the last of the egg whites are stirred in until you have a smooth glossy chocolate mix.
7. Now it's time to add the softly whipped cream. Add a half of the cream to the chocolate mix and stir and finally add the rest of the remaining cream until completely combined.
8. Fill a piping bag with the chocolate mixture and pipe the mousse into glasses.
9. I use small glasses as although the chocolate mousse is light it is very rich.
10. Finish with some fresh fruit and shortbread on the side for a sweet delicious dessert!

*CAN BE MADE GLUTEN FREE

Sweet delicious dessert

Chocolate Tray Bake

INGREDIENTS

185ml Sunflower oil
250g Plain Flour** or use Dove Farm GF Plain flour
80g Cocoa Powder
2 ½ teaspoons baking powder **or Dove Farm GF baking powder
1 teaspoon bicarbonate of soda (Bread soda not baking powder!)
325g Brown Sugar
250ml Buttermilk **
125ml Strong coffee or 4 teaspoons instant coffee dissolved in water not boiling, can even be warm
2 teaspoons vanilla extract
2 large eggs**
1 teaspoon Xanthan gum for GF only****

METHOD

1. Heat oven to 180C/350F/GAS 4.
2. Line the base and sides of a roasting tin with greaseproof paper (I used 13"x9").
3. Combine the flour, cocoa powder, baking powder, bicarbonate of soda and sugar in a large bowl.
4. Whisk oil, buttermilk, coffee, vanilla and eggs together in a jug, then pour the wet ingredients into the dry mix and blend well, getting all the lumps and bumps out. Boom! Batter is done.
5. Pour the mixture into the tin and bake for 30-35 minutes until a skewer inserted into the centre comes out clean.
6. Leave to cool in the tin for at least an hour as this is a very soft sponge.
7. For the Icing: Melt 150g butter in a saucepan or zap in the microwave for about a minute in a microwaveable container. Stir in 200g icing sugar, 4 tablespoons of cocoa powder and 2 tablespoons of milk.
8. The icing will be very very very runny ... don't panic! It will thicken as it cools. (If the icing has set too much, reheat it slightly to make it easier to pour.)
9. Pour the icing over the cake and leave to set. Decorate with the sweets, sprinkles, then cut into squares and devour!!!

Trish's Top Tip

10. Replace the milk for dairy alternative: dairy free milk of your choice but you will have to add 2 teaspoons of lemon juice or two teaspoons of apple cider vinegar to add acidity to the milk. Leave for ten minutes and you have the dairy free buttermilk.
11. Add a binding agent to the cake batter when using gluten free flour. The wetter the batter the better for GF bakes. As a rule of thumb mix 2 teaspoons of xanthan gum for every 500g plain flour.
12. Add 1 teaspoon of Xanthan gum for this recipe.
13. Replacing the egg substitute with any of these: 180g apple sauce, 1 large mashed ripe banana.
14. Flaxegg: ... 1 tablespoon of flaxseed mixed with 3 tablespoons of water for every egg used. Leave sit for ten minutes to create a pulp like eggy mix. In this recipe you will need 2 tablespoons flaxseed.
15. Chia Seeds: 1 tablespoon of chia seeds mixed with 3 tablespoons of water for every egg used. Leave sit for ten minutes to create a pulp like eggy mix. In this recipe you will need 2 tablespoons chia seeds.
16. Replacing butter with melted neutral coconut oil.

*CAN BE MADE GLUTEN FREE

Quickest Ever Coffee Tiramisu

INGREDIENTS

4 tablespoons rum (I use Captain Morgan DARK)
1 packet (20 fingers approx) of sponge fingers.
250g Mascarpone cheese
250ml Softly whipped Cream
200ml Custard (Pre-made to speed thing up!)
2-3 tablespoons Cocoa Powder for decoration
200ml Very strong coffee (Espresso if you can)

METHOD

1. Begin by adding 200ml of strong coffee in a dish and add two tablespoons of the rum, and stir.
2. Next quickly add the sponge fingers one by one, rotating each one as you dip in the coffee bath!
3. What you want are the sponge fingers to be coated in the liquor and not soaked. If soaked the tiramisu will have no structure or texture and will end up sloppy and soggy!
4. Line up the sponge fingers in the dish so you have one bottom layer of sponge fingers.
5. In the meantime, whisk the mascarpone in a bowl or mixer until smooth, then add the custard.
6. Once you have the custard batter blended, stir in the last 2 tablespoons of rum and blend.
7. Finally fold in the whipped cream to the mix so you have a delicious soft mousse.
8. Layer some of the custard cream mousse on top of the sponge fingers and repeat with another layer of dipped fingers and top with last remaining cream filling. Just like a sweet lasagne!!
9. Leave the dish in the fridge overnight to set and develop the flavours and do its "thang".
10. Once chilled sprinkle generously with cocoa powder and it's ready to serve!

Quick & tasty!

Delicate French Crêpe

INGREDIENTS
3 Large Eggs
125g Plain flour or Gluten Free
290ml Low fat milk
2 tablespoons Sunflower oil
2 teaspoon sugar

SUGGESTED FILLINGS
Nutella
Nutella, banana, greek yoghurt and honey
Lemon and Sugar
Mixed fruit, greek yoghurt and honey
Sliced ham and grated cheese
Smoked salmon, cream cheese and chives
Cream cheese and parma ham

METHOD

1. Sieve the flour into a large bowl and add the eggs and stir.
2. Slowly whisk the eggs stir until you have a smooth paste.
3. Next add the milk gradually so you don't end up with lumps in the batter.
4. Sprinkle in the sugar (it doesn't really matter what stage you add the sugar).
5. Finish the batter by adding two tablespoons of oil (this helps prevent the crepe from sticking).
6. Leave the batter rest in the fridge for 20 minutes and then take out of the fridge and leave at room temperature for ten minutes to develop the gluten.
7. I use a French crepe machine but any non stick frying pan will do.
8. Approximately 60ml will make a 10" crepe and 80ml for a 12" crêpe.
9. Two ladles gave me the perfect size for my machine so experiment with what works for you depending on the size of pan or machine you have.
10. Grease the pan or machine with about a teaspoon of butter while you preheat. It's important to pre-heat the pan because if the pan isn't hot enough the batter will stick.
11. Scoop about two ladles of batter into the centre of the frying pan (if using) and swirl until the batter fits the frying pan or if using a crêpe machine smooth batter into a circular motion using the batter spreader provided.
12. The crêpes cook pretty quickly so keep an eye on them. The batter begins to brown from the edges in. Wait until you can see a lovely golden hue from the edges and gently lift to take a sneak peek. The paler the crêpe the softer the crepe.
13. Remember the crêpe will continue to cook on either side once you flip so don't overcook it. They are also very delicate and not as robust as a pancake so just be gentle.
14. Once you flip the crêpe, have your fillings ready. I smear with a little Nutella, fold the crêpe in half while still on the pan and repeat the filling and fold once more.
15. Remove and serve immediately with fresh fruit or greek yoghurt/cream and sprinkled on icing sugar and boom your done!
16. Delicate delicious fresh crêpes. Fillings can be as adventurous as you dare! Make them savoury or sweet. The choice is yours! Bon Appétit!

*CAN BE MADE GLUTEN FREE

Bon Appetit!

Flapjack Jammy Oat Bars*

INGREDIENTS

125g Maple syrup (or honey)
100g Coconut oil
200g Porridge oats (can be GF)
50g Ground almonds (optional)
75g Coconut (optional)
½ teaspoon Almond extract (optional)

FRUIT FILLING

200g frozen raspberries (or blueberries or mixed fruit)
1 teaspoon honey (or maple syrup)

METHOD

1. Pre-heat the oven to 180C/350F/Gas4 and grease a 8 x 8 casserole dish with coconut oil. (No need to line as the bars come easily away once baked).
2. In a small saucepan melt the maple syrup (or honey) along with the coconut oil until fully melted.
3. Add the dry ingredients to a bowl and blend. Next stir in the melted wet mix.
4. Pour two thirds of the oatmeal mix and compress into the baking or casserole dish. Flatten using the back a spoon or spatula. You're creating the base for the bars so compressing it helps it combine and stick together.
5. Now put the dish in the oven for a minute or two in the oven to warm the mix. (This helps warm up the oats and make them easier to soak in the fruit mixture).
6. While you're waiting for the oat mix to heat up in the oven, put 200g of the fruit into the same small saucepan to save washing up!
7. Add one teaspoon of honey or maple syrup and bring the fruit mix to the boil. It doesn't take very long, about a minute or two.
8. The frozen fruit mix will start to soften and the fruit is sweetened by the honey or maple syrup.
9. Take the fruit mix off the heat when it comes to the boil. If using all raspberries, taste to see if you need to add a little more honey or a tablespoon of sugar to cut through the sharpness of the raspberries. This really depends on how sharp you like the bars. No need to do this for blueberries as they are sweet enough already.
10. Bake in a pre-heated oven for 20 minutes and no longer.
11. Once the bars are warm, cut into 9 squares are smaller if you want them to last longer! Leave go cold before you attempt to remove as they are fragile. Gorgeous with a scoop of ice cream.
12. These bars are delicious made with any frozen fruit.

CAN BE MADE GLUTEN FREE

102

Easy Peasy Granola Bars*

INGREDIENTS

200g Oats or Gluten Free
50g Almonds (Coarsely chopped)
90g Honey
40g Butter
40g Dark Brown sugar
½ teaspoon vanilla extract
50g Cranberries
40g Dark chocolate

METHOD

1. Preheat oven to 180C/350F/Gas 4.
2. Put the oats and almond in a shallow tray and bake for 5 minutes in a preheated oven.
3. Give them a shake and bake for another 5 minutes. This brings out the natural oils of the almond and the nuttiness of the oats. Transfer to a large bowl to cool for about 5minutes.
4. Put butter, honey and brown sugar into a saucepan and melt until sugar and butter have dissolved, then add the vanilla extract.
5. Pour the cooled butter mixture on top of the oat and nut mix. At this stage throw in the dried cranberries and chocolate chips (reserve a few chips for decoration).
6. Don't worry if the chocolate chips start to melt a little, they turn into delicious glue to keep the bar together.
7. Transfer the oat mixture into either a lined tin or buttered foil tray. I used a 9" square disposable tin. Use the back of a spoon to firmly press the mixture into the pan. You need to press down so the bars stay together once cooled. Scatter a few of the remaining chips and again press into the mixture.
8. Chill for at least an hour and cut into 12 bars. If you prefer a softer bite let the bars at room temp.

*CAN BE MADE GLUTEN FREE

Pop the kettle on!

Crunchie Honeycomb

INGREDIENTS
100g Caster Sugar
85g Golden Syrup
1 ½ teaspoons Bicarbonate of soda

METHOD

1. First get everything together and in place as this is a very quick recipe so you need your wits about you....
2. Weigh up the sugar.
3. Weigh up the golden syrup.
4. Measure out the bicarbonate of soda.
5. Get the whisk ready.
6. Get the spatula ready.
7. Prepare the tray. Line with a silicone sheet or non-stick parchment.
8. Jump up and down and get excited as you're ready to make some HONEYCOMB.
9. Put the sugar and golden syrup into the pot and stir very gently over a low heat until the sugar has melted.
10. It will turn to a lovely golden honey goo. Now turn the heat up a little and it will start to bubble around the edge of the saucepan and slowly change colour. Now set the timer for three minutes or if you have a sugar thermometer it should be at soft ball stage at 112C.
11. The minute it hits the soft ball temperature turn off the heat.
12. Immediately sprinkle the bicarbonate of soda on top and whisk ... whisk again like you did last summer. LOL!
13. Pour the delicious molten golden honeycomb directly onto the prepared tray.
14. Now leave the honeycomb to set, it takes 30 minutes to harden.
15. Once set, give it a gentle smash and it will break into golden honey goodness.
16. Coat with chocolate and you have just made "Honeycomb".

Ka-boom!

Mango & Passion Fruit Ice-cream

INGREDIENTS

285g Tropical smoothie mix (Pineapple, Papaya and Mango prepared mix)
2 Medium bananas (Sliced and then frozen overnight)
100g Mango and passion fruit yoghurt
Juice of one large orange
100ml of Passion and Mango fruit coulis

METHOD

1. Use a food processor with a blade attachment.
2. Transfer the frozen chopped banana and smoothie mix to the food processor. Add the orange juice followed by the yoghurt and blend.
3. This will take a few minutes as you want all the frozen fruit to blend to a soft smooth cream.
4. Stop the food processor a few times and using a spatula, scrape down the sides to make sure all the lumps and bumps of frozen fruit get mixed through.
5. You will then have a beautiful smooth ice-cream ready to freeze in an ice-cream machine or pour into a tupperware container and freeze for a couple of hours.
6. If you wish, the mixture can also be poured into some silicone ice cream popsicle mounds and set overnight then dipped in Belgian chocolate of your choice and sprinkled with some freeze dried passion fruit. A delicious healthier ice-cream magnum.
7. This is not a soft scoop ice-cream so you will need to let it thaw a little before you can use an ice-cream scoop. Dip the ice-cream scoop in warm water as it makes gliding over the ice cream easier to serve.
8. I use the smallest of my ice-cream scoops to scoop individual ice-cream balls, then I place them on a silicone mat and open freeze for an hour.
9. Once frozen in shape, I can then pop the ice-cream balls in a freezer bag to have at hand for any ice-cream emergency!
10. They are perfect for kids - fast, quick, easy and no mess. These little balls of ice cream are delicious dipped in white chocolate and leave to set so you have an ice cream chocolate bomb. Serve with fresh fruit.
11. Using a baby ice-cream scoop also makes it easier for portion control as each scoop weighs 15g and is perfect for tiny tots.

Trish's Top Tip

Using the above recipe is just a guideline. Use frozen raspberries or mixed frozen berries with your favourite yoghurt. Add some honey instead of orange juice. Experiment with different coulis and you have your very own variety of ice-cream!

Chill out and enjoy!

Fluffiest Marshmallow Ever

STEP 1
3 x Sachets of Gelatine (12g sachet each)
200g/ml water
3 teaspoons vanilla extract

STEP 2
400g Caster sugar
250g Glucose syrup (Golden syrup will do)
60ml water

DUSTING
200g Icing sugar
100g Cornflour

DECORATING (OPTIONAL)
5g Dried freeze raspberries
5g Dried freeze sour cherries
5g Dried passion fruit
100g White chocolate
100g Milk chocolate
100g 55% Dark chocolate

METHOD
1. Double line and oil a 9" x 13" baking tray with clingfilm.
2. Clingfilm must be oiled to prevent the marshmallow from sticking. Overlap with clingfilm if necessary.

STEP 1
3. Put 200ml of water and the vanilla extract in the stand alone mixing bowl.
4. Sprinkle the three sachets directly on top of the water mix and let bloom for 10 minutes.

STEP 2
5. Pour 60ml of water into a medium sized pot. Sprinkle in the 400g of sugar and finally pour 250g of glucose syrup.
6. Give the sugar mixture a good stir and then using a pastry brush, run around the bottom rim of the saucepan to dissolve any sugar sticking to the pot. This helps to prevent the sugar from crystallising.
7. Now leave the mixture slowly come to a boil. Once it boils set the timer for approximately a minute. Using a sugar thermometer it should read 112C-115C. If you don't have a sugar thermometer it normally takes just a minute to bring it to soft ball stage. To check take a tiny teaspoon and plop into very cold water and it should leave a little glucose putty on the teaspoon.
8. Once the sugar syrup has come to correct temperature swiftly take it off the heat and pour directly on the gelatine mix. It will foam up immediately like bubble soup!
9. Start the mixer slowly and bring it up to the highest speed and keep whisking for ten minutes.
10. At first it looks honey in colour but that changes as the air is whipped and the sugar starts to take on volume and whips to a delicious white silky foam.
11. Once the ten minutes of whisking is up the whipped marshmallow is now ready for moulding.
12. Using an oiled spatula scoop out the fluffy marshmallow mix to the prepared tin and paddle out the mixture to the corners and smooth the top.
13. Using a sieve, dust liberally some icing sugar and coat the whole tin with icing sugar before you cover with a thin film of clingfilm. This stops the marshmallow from forming a skin.
14. Leave the marshmallow mixture for 6 hours to set or ideally overnight.
15. Once set, using an oiled knife, cut the marshmallows into bitesize portions.
16. Blend 200g of icing sugar and 100g cornflour into a bowl and stir the marshmallows gently coating them with the cornflour and icing sugar blend.
17. You can now dip your marshmallows in a variety of melted chocolate and sprinkle some with freeze dried fruits or just leave plain!

Meringues

INGREDIENTS

4 Egg whites (Large, approx 155g in weight)
¼ teaspoon cream of tartar
120g Caster Sugar
120 Icing Sugar
½ teaspoon vanilla extract (Optional)**

METHOD

1. Preheat the oven to 100C or ¼ gas.
2. Line a tray with a silicone mat or non stick mat or rice paper... not greaseproof as the meringue will stick.
3. Make sure the mixing bowl is sparkling clean. I add a few drops of squeezed lemon to the bowl and wipe clean with a paper towel before I start. I do the same with the whisk attachment.
4. Place the egg whites in the mixing bowl and whip the egg whites until foamy. This will take a few minutes.
5. Wait until the egg whites start to get white and foamy and have a soft whip before you add the cream of tartar to help stabilise that delicious whip.
6. When you see the egg white getting whiter, slow the mixer now and add the caster sugar slowly.
7. When all the caster sugar has been added, turn the mixer up to whip until the meringue is nearly glossy and then add the remaining icing sugar. Again slowly, now add the vanilla extract or flavouring of choice and whip until very stiff.
8. You should now be able to put the bowl over your head and the mixture will stay. If the mixture is too soft you'll have it on your head!!
9. At this stage you can add freeze dried fruit sprinkled into the meringue mixture and swirled through.
10. Transfer the meringue to a clean piping bag fitted with a nozzle and pipe or dollops mounds of meringue into blobs on the silicon mat.
11. Bake the meringues at 100C for 1 hour if little meringues or 1 ½-2 hours depending on the size.
12. Once baked turn off the oven and leave them dry out in the oven until cool.

Clean as you go!

Mixed Berry Smoothie

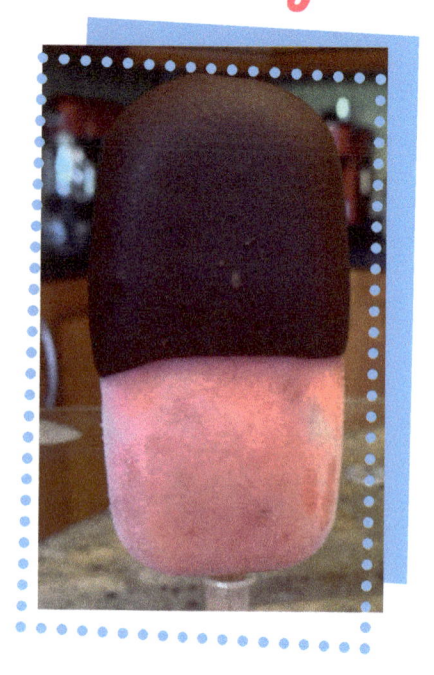

INGREDIENTS
200g Frozen Berries
250ml Orange juice
100g Yoghurt of your choice
2 tablespoons of honey (30ml)
1 Banana

METHOD

1. Start with the liquids first so it doesn't stick at the bottom of the blender.
2. Pour the orange juice, the delicious liquid sunshine into the blender first.
3. Next pour in the yoghurt, whatever flavour tickles your fancy.
4. Tip in the frozen fruit
5. Break up the banana and add to the mix.
6. Finally squeeze or pour in the honey.
7. Put the lid on the blender and secure in place unless you want to redecorate the kitchen!!
8. Lucky for me I use the Kmix so it has a frozen pulse option. Just press and blend for a few minutes and you'll have the most psychedelic fruit smoothie! It would nearly glow in the dark with all it's goodness!
9. Now pour into a glass and enjoy.

Alternative Tips

10. Fill an ice cream tray with the smoothie mix and when frozen you can plip plop into a cold glass of milk and see the colour change to a "pink milk". Kids love it!
11. Fill a silicone flexi ice cream mould with the delicious smoothie and allow to freeze solid. They easily pop out of the mould. Once frozen dip into melted chocolate and sprinkle with nuts if you choose for your own magnum style smoothie pop.
12. Pour into an ice cream type Calypso mould and push pops are yours in the making!!
13. You can mix flavours, you can add juices, smoothies you name it and get creative!

Overnight Apple & Cinnamon Porridge Oats

INGREDIENTS

200g Traditional porridge oats or GF**
180ml low fat milk (or almond/oat/unsweetened) or Dairy free alternative**
270g Brambly Apple sauce (gives a sharp bite and helps enhance the apple flavour)
2 Full eggs ** or one flax egg and one mashed banana for vegan**
50g Dark Brown sugar (or 50ml of maple syrup or honey)**
2 teaspoons vanilla Extract
2 teaspoons Cinnamon
½ teaspoon Baking powder or GF**
400g Chopped Apple (I used tinned for speed but brambly apples are perfect too!) **SEE TIP

METHOD

1. Put all the dry ingredients into a bowl and blend.
2. Whisk all the wet ingredients into a jug.
3. Lightly butter a casserole dish (mine is approx 7x 11").
4. Blend the wet with the dry until completely mixed through.
5. Pout into the buttered casserole dish and spread out the mixture.
6. Cover with some clingfilm and leave rest overnight in the fridge.
7. Pre-heat the oven the next morning to 180C.
8. Remove the dish from the fridge.
9. Bake until golden on top for about 30-35 minutes.
10. Rest on a cooling rack for 5 minutes before serving.
11. Delicious with a dribble of maple syrup, scattered fruit and an extra dollop of greek yoghurt!
12. Scrumdiddledeeumptious!!

(Make a Flax egg -1 tablespoon flaxseed mixed with three tablespoons of water).
Change the apple to frozen mixed berry, or raspberries or blueberries.
If using frozen fruit just make sure you gently mix the fruit at the last stage, or the porridge could turn violet.
Can add 50g chopped nuts too.

**Trish's Top Tip

Can be made gluten free by changing to GF Oats and baking powder.
Can be made vegan by replacing sugar with 50ml maple syrup and/or daily free milk of choice.
One Flax egg and one mashed banana instead of eggs.

#Scrumdiddledeeumptious

P.p.p.p.p.... Penguin Sponge Cake!

INGREDIENTS
320g Crushed 'PENGUIN' biscuits
250ml Milk (I used low fat)
2 teaspoons baking powder
30g Belgian chocolate chips 55% (Optional)

TOPPING
Chocolate spread
Malteesers

METHOD

1. Pre-heat the oven to 180C/350F/Gas 4 and line a small brownie tin (I used a 6.5" square tray).
2. Blitz the biscuits in a food processor until you have a fine crumb.
3. If you don't have a food processor crush the biscuits using a rolling pin and place the biscuits in a ziplock bag and hammer the daylights out of the biscuits until you have fine biscuit crumbs.
4. Warm the milk so it's not too hot and not too cold.... Just like goldilocks, just right!
5. Sprinkle the baking soda on top of the biscuits and mix well.
6. Add the warm milk in on top of the crushed biscuits and stir until completely blended so you have no lumps or bumps.
7. Pour the very wet batter into a lined tin and bake in a preheated oven at 180C for 20/25 minutes
8. Once cool, this cake is a very soft and delicate sponge so be gentle when handling.
9. Cover with whatever topping you would like and cut into squares. Serve with ice-cream and a drizzle of caramel sauce.

CAN BE MADE GLUTEN FREE- Sub to GF biscuits and baking powder add ½ teaspoon Xanthan gum

Add ice-cream #PerfectMatch

Strawberry Cheesecake No-Bake

INGREDIENTS
1 Sachet of Dr. Oetker Gelatine (12g)
1 Sachet Hartley Sugar Free Strawberry flavour jelly (11.5g)
150ml Water

BISCUIT BASE (STEP 2)
225g Digestive Biscuits
120g Butter
30g Caster Sugar

STRAWBERRY FILLING (STEP 3)
200g Cream cheese
135g Caster sugar
300ml Cream
250g Mascarpone Cheese
2 tablespoons fresh lemon juice (Optional)
450g Puréed Strawberries (I used frozen)
20g Vera Miklas freeze dried strawberries (Optional - Blitzed to a powder in food processor)
DECORATION
250g Fresh strawberries
150ml Whipped cream

STEP 1 (GELATINE MIX)
1. Weigh our 150ml of cold water in a bowl.
2. Sprinkle the strawberry jelly and gelatine sachets over the cold water.
3. Leave to bloom for ten minutes until it soaks up all the water.

STEP 2
4. Prepare a 9" round loose bottom tin. Grease the base with butter and line the sides only with parchment paper. This make life so much easier when removing the cheesecake. Trust me!
5. Melt the butter and let it cool as you crush the digestive biscuits.
6. Crush the biscuits either by putting into a freezer bag and using a rolling pin to crush or by blitzing in a food processor. Pulse into fine breadcrumbs. I use the latter method as it's faster.
7. Pour the melted butter over the biscuit and blend well.
8. Press the biscuit crumb into the tin and chill for at least 15 minutes.

STEP 3
9. Add 20g of dried strawberries to the food processor and blitz to a fine powder. Now add the strawberries to the dried powder (if using) and purée until smooth. Strain through a sieve to get any lumps or bumps out. Set aside.
10. In the mixer add the cream cheese and caster sugar and beat on a medium speed for 2 minutes until fluffy and smooth. Scrape down the bowl if necessary.
11. Add the cream slowly into the mix and beat to a soft whip. This takes about 3 minutes.
12. Stop the mixer and now add the mascarpone and blend until smooth.
13. Pour in the lemon juice followed by the prepared strawberry purée.
14. Microwave gelatine mix for 30-35 seconds making sure it's completely dissolved until the liquid looks clear.
15. Now pour the gelatine mix slowly into the cheesecake filling until completely combined.
16. Once mixed pour the cheesecake filling onto the prepared tin and chill overnight.
17. Once chilled, decorate with some piped whipped cream rosettes and fresh strawberries.

Tooty Fruity Traybake

INGREDIENTS

180ml Milk or Buttermilk
180ml Sunflower oil
2 large eggs
2 teaspoon vanilla extract
300g Self-Raising Flour
140g Caster sugar
2 teaspoon baking powder
100g Porridge oats
200g Frozen berries** or fresh if seasonal (See Tip**)

METHOD

1. First pre-heat the oven to 180C/350F/Gas 4.
2. Line and grease the swiss roll tray or 13" x 9".
3. Measure out all the ingredients so you have everything at hand.
4. Mix the milk, sunflower oil, egg and vanilla extract in a jug.
5. In a separate bowl add the flour, baking powder and oats.
6. Toss the berries into the flour mix before you add the sugar.
7. Add the wet ingredients to dry ingredients and gently stir. Blend but don't over mix as you want to be as light as fairy wings!
8. Pour the batter into a greased and lined swissroll tin about 13" x 9".
9. Sprinkle a little pinch of oats on top for the crunch before they bake.
10. Bake in the preheated oven for about 30 minutes.
11. Remove from tray and cool on baking rack for 10 minutes.
12. Leave for at least 15 minutes to cool as the fruit is very hot and will burn your mouth!! You have to be patient, they're worth the wait.
13. Lash on the glacé icing either with a palette knife or pipe in a zig zag fashion using a piping bag.

ICING GLAZE

14. 200g Icing sugar
15. 2 tablespoons of water
16. (Add water to icing and stir for desired thickness)

Trish's Top Tip

Toss the frozen berries in flour before you mix in the rest of the ingredients so they won't sink to the bottom

Worth the wait!

Waffly Versatile

METHOD

1. Pre-heat the waffle iron. Once hot you must slather in melted butter or the waffle will stick. Years of experience having this Russell Hobbs Waffle machine!! **
2. Mix all the wet ingredients together in a jug to make it easier to pour.
3. Mix all the dry ingredients together.
4. Now combine the wet into the dry ingredients and blend until completely combined.
5. You will have a sloppy batter perfect for the waffle iron or a greased frying pan.
6. It takes 6 minutes for a soft waffle or 8 minutes for an little extra crunch (I love the extra two minutes for a crispy shell).
7. Dust with icing sugar or top with your favourite yoghurt and fresh fruit with a drizzle of honey and sprinkle of nuts.
8. This batter is very versatile. You can add dried or fresh herbs to the batter to make them savoury, add chopped pieces of cooked bacon. The list is endless! Get creative.. they are WAFFLY VERSATILE.

** This is not a paid or promotional post. It is my honest opinion of a great product that has got a hammering over the years with my family of six and still smiling! ... the machine, just like me, waffles on ....

WHOLEWHEAT WAFFLES (SERVES 8 OR ONE HUNGRY TEENAGER)

260g Wholewheat Flour (or porridge oats GF blitzed in processor)
3 tsp baking powder
½ teaspoon cinnamon
2 large eggs
100ml Sunflower oil
2 tablespoons of brown sugar
420ml Buttermilk
1 teaspoon vanilla extract

VANILLA WAFFLES (SERVES 8 OR ONE HUNGRY TEENAGER)

300g Self-raising Flour
2 tsp baking powder
½ teaspoon cinnamon
2 Large eggs
100ml Sunflower oil
2 tablespoons Caster sugar
300ml Milk (low fat)
1 teaspoon vanilla extract

Waffles on!

Lightning Source UK Ltd.
Milton Keynes UK
UKHW050437080621
385090UK00003B/109